THE SECOND
RECONSTRUCTION
A HISTORY OF THE MODERN
CIVIL RIGHTS MOVEMENT

by
Gary A. Donaldson

AN ANVIL ORIGINAL
under the general editorship of
Hans L. Trefousse

KRIEGER PUBLISHING COMPANY
MALABAR, FLORIDA
2000

Original Edition   2000

Printed and Published by
KRIEGER PUBLISHING COMPANY
KRIEGER DRIVE
MALABAR, FLORIDA 32950

FROM A DECLARATION OF PRINCIPLES JOINTLY ADOPTED BY A COMMITTEE OF THE AMERICAN BAR ASSOCIATION AND A COMMITTEE OF PUBLISHERS:
This publication is designed to provide accurate and authoritative information in regard to the subject matter covered. It is sold with the understanding that the publisher is not engaged in rendering legal, accounting, or other professional service. If legal advice or other expert assistance is required, the services of a competent professional person should be sought.

Library of Congress Cataloging-In-Publication Data

Donaldson, Gary.
    The second Reconstruction : a history of the modern civil rights movement / by Gary A. Donaldson. — Original ed.
      p. cm. — (The anvil series)
    "An Anvil original."
    Includes bibliographical references and index.
    ISBN 1-57524-066-1 (pbk. : alk. paper)
    1. Afro-Americans—Civil rights—History—20th century. 2. Civil rights movements—United States—History—20th century. 3. United States—Race relations. 4. Afro-Americans—Civil rights—History—20th century Sources.
5. Civil rights movements—United States—History—20th century Sources.
6. United States—Race relations Sources. I. Title.
E185.61.D65 2000
973'.0496073—dc21
                            99–31735
                              CIP

10 9 8 7 6 5 4 3 2

CONTENTS

INTRODUCTION

The First Reconstruction began immediately following the Civil War and lasted in some areas of the South until as late as 1877. It was a plan designed by the federal government to bring the defeated South back into the Union, and through legislation, manage and regulate race relations in the Old Confederacy. Instead, Reconstruction became the basis of a social upheaval and a national political realignment, aspects of which could still be felt in the social and political fiber of the nation well into the second half of the next century. For the newly freed slaves, supposedly a primary benefactor of federal legislation in this period, post-Civil War Reconstruction was a dismal failure. Free but unequal and poverty stricken, the freed slaves became a political and economic threat to white southerners, while they were, at the same time, extremely vulnerable because of their economic condition. The result was, by the turn of the twentieth century, a white controlled South, legal segregation of the two races, a consenting federal government, and a nearly complete political disenfranchisement of African Americans. That state of affairs continued until after World War II, when things began to change rapidly for black Americans.

The Second Reconstruction was born out of the first. After some seventy years of passive neglect and complicity in the southern suppression of blacks, the federal government, for a number of reasons, again attempted to regulate race relations in the South through legislation. The move was primarily politically motivated, and generally in response to demands from the African American community, now newly empowered by their numbers, their new economic standing, and their political clout. Running parallel were also a series of outside forces that pushed the federal government to bring its powers to bear in an effort to end racial injustices in the South. The Cold War had a major impact on the federal government's need to see that blacks in America were given, at least, equal opportunity under the law; the newly independent African states threatened to slip into the Soviet sphere of influence in response to American racism. Also, the atrocities committed by Nazi Germany made Americans acutely aware of the consequences of racism. So it was not only internal forces that brought the U.S. government to give its tacit support to the demands of American blacks in the decades after World War II.

The Second Reconstruction was a grassroots movement, led primarily by African American community leaders, organized most often at the local level, and supported by the black masses. Although the federal government was always a prominent force, it was a reluctant one, often a follower in the movement rather than a leader of it.

The question arises, was the modern civil rights movement of the sixties a success? The answer, of course, depends on the objectives. What was ventured determines the success of the gains. If the civil rights movement intended to bring an end to legal segregation and disenfranchisement of African Americans in the South, it was a rousing success. By the mid-1960s that feat had been accomplished. If, however, the objective was to end racial discrimination and achieve racial equality in the nation, the civil rights movement has not succeeded, and, in that context, it continues on.

This small book intends to chart and interpret the modern civil rights movement from the end of World War II, when the promises of racial equality were great, to the end of the century, when race relations in America, by most accounts, had reached a low ebb. There is, however, hope in a growing black middle class, the real beneficiaries of the civil rights movement. In between these dates there were highs and lows, successes and failures, advances and backlashes. And it changed America.

 THE ANVIL SERIES

Anvil paperbacks give an original analysis of a major field of history or a problem area, drawing upon the most recent research. They present a concise treatment and can act as supplementary material for college history courses. Written by many of the outstanding historians in the United States, the format is one-half narrative text, one-half supporting documents, often from hard to find sources.

PART I

THE SECOND RECONSTRUCTION

CHAPTER 1

A SEEDTIME FOR REFORM

The Great Migration North. World War II, not unlike the Civil War, unleashed a whole series of social, political, and economic changes in America. Blacks, after 1945, would stand at the center of many of those changes. It was a time when the nation's will came together with the means to tear down racial barriers, and to begin the long and arduous journey down the long road to racial equality. For African Americans, it was a time of great hope and anticipation. It was the beginning of the Second Reconstruction, the beginning of the modern civil rights movement.

But getting to that point, where hopes and dreams for the first time seemed achievable, had been difficult. Just fifty years before, during the last decade of the nineteenth century, African Americans found themselves with little hope for their future. Segregated from the white population and disenfranchised by law, they had been forced into a kind of peonage that kept them where white southerners wanted them, powerless, subdued, "in their place." There was only one method of protest available: migrate, leave the South and move to the North where opportunities might be better. The result was the Great Migration, an event that made possible the modern civil rights movement.

At the turn of the twentieth century at least 90 percent of all African Americans lived in the South, the vast majority on farms as poor tenant farmers or sharecroppers. The migration of blacks north began to show up in census and statistical reports as early as the 1890s. And it is no coincidence that it was during the next twenty years, as the migrations increased, that race relations in the South reached their lowest point in American history. In those twenty years, 200,000 African Americans protested the deplorable situation in the South by migrating to urban centers in the North. In the next decade another half million made the trip, most hoping to secure wartime jobs in an expanding northern economy. In the 1920s, 750,000 left the South for opportunities in the North, many pushed off their southern tenant farms by the mechanization of cotton agriculture during the decade. The migrations slowed during the years of the Great Depression, but picked up again as war clouds formed at the very end of the thirties. During the decade of the

1940s, one million African Americans moved out of the South looking for wartime jobs, a large number of those finding opportunities in California. Many were pushed off the land by further farm mechanization, especially by the invention of the cotton-picking machine which was put into wide use in the South during the decade.

While this movement was reaching its peak near midcentury, the American South itself was in the midst of changes that would have an impact on the postwar civil rights movement. Agriculture, once by far the dominant force in the southern economy, was, just before World War II, beginning to give way to a new and vibrant industrial development. The result was that the power structure in this New South was beginning a slow but certain shift from the old landed gentry to a new and prosperous urban elite composed mostly of professionals employed by absentee owned corporations. Millions of white-collar employees, many from the North, filled the employment ranks and populated the growing cities, people with little interest in perpetuating the old social system. Through the forties, fifties, and sixties the southern cotton culture, and its accompanying outdated racial mores, dominated less and less of southern society. By the 1960s most New South cities contained a moderate element, usually composed of forward-looking businessmen who often despised the image of the South as America's racist backwater, an image that strangled northern investment. This group would play a moderating force at several junctures during the civil rights movement.

Those African Americans who moved north received the right to vote, and for the first time since the First Reconstruction African Americans could cast their votes in numbers significant enough to influence elections. The jobs that African Americans wanted were primarily in the large, industrial cities in the North, Northeast, and Far West. These cities were almost always located in states with the largest electoral votes. Between 1940 and 1947, the number of African Americans in New York City grew from 100,000 to over 800,000; in Chicago from 300,000 to 420,000; in Philadelphia from 300,000 to 415,000; and in Los Angeles from 100,000 to 210,000. In many areas of the North and West, African Americans, by the end of the war, held the balance of political power. By the late 1940s African American voters in the North were making a difference in local, state, and federal elections. The migration, and the political power it brought, would be one significant aspect of the advances African Americans would make in the postwar period.

Say Farewell to the Party of Lincoln. It was during the presidency of Franklin Delano Roosevelt that blacks for the first time put to use their newfound political clout. The political power structure of the thirties and forties, however, still worked against African Americans. In almost every situation, FDR was forced to defer to the demands of powerful southern congressmen in his own party over any appeals for black civil rights. Southern racist demagogues like Senator Theodore Bilbo, Representative John Rankin, both Mississippi Democrats, and Georgia Senator Herman Talmadge wielded so much power in the halls of Congress that not even Roosevelt could influence the course of government without their support. To engage these powerful congressmen in battle over the social issues of civil rights would be to lose their support in other areas, areas that Roosevelt deemed much more important, such as New Deal legislation and his foreign policy initiatives. At the same time, these powerful southern congressmen believed they had been elected to protect the southern system of segregation and disenfranchisement. This dilemma, of having to placate both southern congressmen and African Americans, would plague the Democratic leadership for at least two more decades.

The southern wing of the Democratic party also proved to be a dilemma for African Americans. Blacks wanted to support FDR and the New Deal, but they were reluctant to leave their beloved Party of Lincoln to follow a party that harbored racists like Talmadge, Rankin, and Bilbo. FDR's New Deal, however, aided African Americans through the depression and gave black workers jobs during the war. Despite the racist element in the Democratic party, African Americans voted in large numbers for Roosevelt—the leader of the party that seemed to be doing the most to aid their plight. In 1932, only 21 percent of the African American vote went to Roosevelt. But four years later that number jumped to 75 percent in one of the most dramatic voter shifts in American history. In 1940, the numbers declined after a valiant attempt by the Republicans to bring blacks back into their party, but still 67 percent of America's blacks supported FDR.

African Americans supported Roosevelt because New Deal programs offered them some relief from the depths of the depression, but the New Deal did little to further the cause of civil rights for African Americans. In fact, most New Deal programs continued to impose segregation and discrimination as government policy. Civilian Conservation Corps (CCC) camps, for instance, were strictly segregated, as were most Tennessee Valley Authority (TVA) projects. The National Recovery Administration (NRA), dubbed "Negroes Ruined Again" by some African American leaders, authorized lower pay scales for blacks. And the Federal Housing Authority (FHA) upheld race-based restrictive covenants in housing. Despite the segregation and discrimination, however, African Americans did receive TVA jobs and were welcomed into CCC camps; they also received an increased working wage as a result of the NRA, and they were able to buy houses under FHA programs, opportunities denied them before. Clearly, African Americans did not receive their fair share of the New Deal, but their condition improved considerably as a result of the programs.

The New Deal went a long way toward bringing African Americans into the Democratic party, but there were other reasons why blacks supported FDR. Roosevelt often named black leaders to federal posts, and many of his appointments to New Deal agencies were sensitive to African American issues. In 1935 the black educator Mary McLeod Bethune was named by FDR as his special advisor on minority affairs. A year later she was appointed director of the Division of Negro Affairs of the National Youth Administration (NYA). Through her efforts, African Americans received a significant portion of NYA funds. The Interior Department, under its Secretary Harold Ickes, became the home of the much-publicized "Black Kitchen Cabinet." Ickes, a strong supporter of civil rights, appointed a number of black Americans to important positions in his department, including Clark Foreman, Robert C. Weaver, and William H. Hastie. Throughout the 1930s and 1940s, this assemblage formed a pressure group that pushed the administration to end various aspects of segregation. Ickes also poured federal money into black schools and hospitals in the South. For the first time in American history, African American leaders had at least some input into the federal governmental process.

Roosevelt also worked to liberalize the Supreme Court, and, as black Americans saw it, that served the cause of civil rights and further endeared FDR to the African American community. Before 1937 the court was primarily conservative, reflecting appointments made by Republican presidents in the 1920s. This conservative-dominated court blocked civil rights initiatives by finding almost exclusively for states' rights in civil rights matters. In 1935, for instance, the court, in *Grovey v. Townsend*, affirmed the legality of the white primary. After 1937, however, FDR was able to appoint five justices to the court, including the important liberals Hugo Black and William O. Douglas. The result was a more liberal court and a number of positive decisions on civil rights. In 1944, the court overturned *Grovey v. Townsend*, and in *Smith v. Allright* it concluded that African Americans could not be excluded from voting in state primaries. *Smith v. Allright* paved the way for the civil rights court battles of the next decade.

Another reason African Americans supported the New Deal was the actions and attitude of the president's wife. Eleanor Roosevelt was in the unique position of being able to support civil rights without subjecting her husband to the political liabilities associated with that cause. Throughout her husband's presidency, Mrs. Roosevelt was the official ombudsman for African Americans, and associated herself often and openly with African American leaders and African American associations.

Those blacks who migrated north also found themselves drawn to the Democrats because of the impact of organized labor. By 1936, labor unions had forged a power base inside the New Deal coalition and the Democratic party. Black migrants to the North usually found work in factories, where they joined unions. Increasingly, these workers became proletarian in their social, economic, and political outlook. Not surprisingly, black Americans living in the North and working in factories soon came to associate their situation more with the American factory worker, and thus the Democratic party, than with the ancient problems of Jim Crow and the Old South.

For all of these reasons, the vast majority of northern urban African Americans, by the end of World War II, no longer associated with the party of Lincoln; they saw their future in the party of American labor and American liberalism—the Democrats, and that shift in allegiance would change the character of American politics in the last half of the twentieth century.

The Election of 1940 and the Discovery of Political Power. The New Deal may have aided African Americans during the depression years, but afterward, when the wars in Europe and Asia again fueled American industry and jobs were plentiful, a number of black leaders made it clear that they were not satisfied that FDR had done enough for African Americans. Black labor leader A. Philip Randolph of the Brotherhood of Sleeping Car Porters and Walter White of the National Association for the Advancement of Colored People (NAACP) pushed FDR to make concessions to African Americans as the 1940 election approached. The Republican candidate, Wendell Willkie, made extensive promises to blacks throughout the campaign, and the Republican party platform called for significant concessions to African Americans. The Democratic party platform, in contrast, reflected the power of the party's southern wing and thus was weak on civil rights. On October 25, Roosevelt, fearing a significant loss of black votes, finally relented by appointing several African Americans to second-level administrative positions, and announcing the establishment of an army air corps training school for African American pilots at Tuskegee, Alabama. Roosevelt won the election, taking large percentages of black votes in nearly every major city in the North.

The election of 1940 was a foreshadowing of what lay ahead in American politics, particularly for the Democrats. In the 1940 campaign Roosevelt was able to straddle the civil rights issue, either by using his own political abilities, or, more likely, because civil rights was not yet the volatile issue it would become. Pitching only a few fairly insignificant concessions to each side, Roosevelt was able to keep both southern whites and the African Americans in line. In the next two decades American presidents, particularly those in the Democratic party, would find it nearly impossible to please both white southerners and African Americans. The outcome of the 1940 election also made it clear to African Americans for the first time that they were a potentially powerful voting bloc, that they could make demands and receive concessions. In several ways the 1940 election set the stage for the postwar civil rights movement.

Events after the election, however, threw even more light on what was to come. Randolph immediately concluded that FDR's modest preelection concessions were really of little consequence in light of the black support the president had received. In the summer of 1941, Randolph demanded more concessions, and threatened the president with a march on Washington of, he promised, 100,000 black demonstrators if the administration did not give in. Again FDR yielded. He issued Executive Order 8802 which prohibited discriminatory hiring practices by unions and companies with government contacts. It also established a wartime Federal Employment Practices Commission (FEPC) to investigate violations of the president's order. Randolph called off the march.

Randolph's March on Washington (MOW) movement was important

in laying the groundwork for the coming civil rights movement for several reasons. First, it established a new method of mass protest that clearly got the government's attention. Here for the first time in U.S. history an organized, nonviolent, mass protest (or at least the promise of one) had forced the government to concede. This type of direct action would be the primary method used by the next generation of civil rights leaders. Second, the march threat had forced the federal government, again for the first time, to deal with African Americans as a singular pressure group, and to accept their threat of direct action as a potential political liability. African Americans were thought to be generally apathetic toward politics, disorganized, and uncontrollable in any modern political sense. Here, as Randolph had promised it, up to 100,000 African American citizens could be collected at the same place to make demands on the government. A last important point is that Randolph insisted that the MOW would be a blacks-only movement. "There are some things Negroes must do alone," he said. As the civil rights movement of the sixties progressed, a debilitating conflict would emerge between those who believed the movement needed the assistance of white Americans and those who did not.

Despite the demographic shifts that placed African Americans in a position of potential political power, and despite the concessions made by the Roosevelt administration, black civilians generally received little during the war. They had hoped that good jobs in the war industries would allow them to make a place for themselves in the national economy, a place that would be maintained into the postwar period. But they managed to hold only the most menial jobs, and they were the last hired and first fired. Despite the enactment of the FEPC, the federal government continued to allow discrimination in hiring practices when it was demanded by government-contracted employers. In the electrical industry, for instance, African Americans held only about one percent of the jobs, and only three percent in the rubber industry. Both of those industries were almost totally mobilized for war and under government contracts, and no amount of pressure from the FEPC could force either industry to hire African Americans in large numbers.

The situation for those African Americans who had migrated to the North may not have been all they had hoped, but it was infinitely better than the situation in the South. In the North blacks had the vote, and they quickly became a powerful political force in America. They may have faced discrimination in the job market in the North, but the war-time jobs they received provided economic opportunities that African Americans could have barely imagined in the South.

By the war's end it was clear that African Americans would be making demands—on the government, and on society. Their newfound political power was now coupled with a growing economic base. New methods of protest had been tried, and there was a growing racial consciousness, and an increasing interest among blacks in the civil rights movement. Membership in the NAACP, for instance, saw a dramatic expansion during the war.

The war itself brought additional changes. Nearly one million African Americans served in the military, although they did so in segregated units. Their contribution to the war effort added moral justification to their claims of equality. At the same time, the war's end brought the news of the Holocaust, and forced many Americans to examine their beliefs on the question of race, and consider the dangers of racism in America.

World War II was the seedtime for reform. Everything necessary was in place. It would be the war's end that would mark the beginning of modern civil rights movement, the Second Reconstruction in American history.

CHAPTER 2

POSTWAR OPTIMISM

Setting the Stage and Some Early Victories. The end of the war brought tremendous optimism to the African American community; the booming postwar economy promised to raise up African Americans along with the rest of the nation. Fear of a postwar depression evaporated almost immediately as the nation's war machine was switched over to peacetime production in order to meet the growing demand for consumer goods. The Gross National Product (GNP) rose from $206 billion to $285 billion in the decade of the 1940s, with the result that the number of civilian jobs rose from fifty-four million to sixty million in just the first five years after the war. Unleashed wartime savings sent personal expenditures up from 122 million to 195 million in the same period. And black Americans benefited, if only relatively. Median black income rose from $1,614 in 1947 to $2,338 in just five years; and as a percentage of white income, black earnings increased from 41 percent before the war to 57 percent in 1952. When the war ended one million more African Americans had civilian jobs than before Pearl Harbor, and those working in government service jobs had jumped from 60,000 to 300,000.

Jobs meant money, and money meant potential political power. The war's end brought significant financial support to several civil rights organizations and protest groups. The NAACP, still the principal African American organization, increased its numbers dramatically during the war years, showing an apparent growing interest among blacks in the civil rights movement. By 1946 the association had ballooned to 450,000 members from just 50,000 in 1940. Within a year, it had added another 150,000 members with a total of 1,500 branches throughout the country. The NAACP continued to operate in its traditional arenas of litigation, lobbying, and legislation. In 1942, the Congress for Racial Equality (CORE) was organized in Chicago under the leadership of James Farmer. CORE was founded as an interracial organization that experimented with nonviolent direct action as a means of protest. In the first decade after the war, CORE had some success in desegregating lunch counters and movie theaters in the North using nonviolent methods such as picketing and sit-ins.

There were other reasons for optimism at the end of the war. The nation's new internationalist foreign policy seemed to make it clear that America's place in the new world order would suffer severely if the U.S. continued to treat blacks unequally. The primary symbol of that new world order, and American internationalism, was the newly organized United Nations. The first statement from the U.N. was "All human beings are born free and equal in dignity and rights." Walter White, W. E. B. DuBois, and Mary McLeod Bethune had participated in early U.N. organizational meetings as representatives of the NAACP. Ralph Bunche, the grandson of a slave, was named in 1946 to head the U.N.'s Division of Trusteeship. A year later he became secretary of the Palestine Commission.

In addition, over 500,000 African Americans had served in the war, most with distinction. The Tuskegee airmen had been praised in action in North Africa and Italy, and black soldiers had fought alongside white units on an emergency basis in Europe. In past wars, military service had produced more hopes than gains for black Americans, but in World War II black soldiers had been an integral part of America's war effort. African American leaders believed, on that basis alone, that blacks could demand changes after the war.

By the end of the war the stage was set. African Americans had gained considerably from the expansion in jobs and income, from service in the military, and from the political power derived from the northern migrations. Protest organizations were active, new methods of protest had been tried, and in the all-important political arena African Americans were about to grasp the balance of power—and having learned the lessons well from Randolph's successes in the 1940 election, they knew that political power meant concessions. All of this came together in 1945. For the first time in the nation's history black Americans had all the tools and the will necessary to launch an aggressive attack on racism. There was tremendous optimism and hope.

At the same time racism was quickly losing whatever intellectual respectability it once had. Hitler's racism had turned into a European holocaust. Japan, throughout the war, had used examples of racism in the United States as propaganda to win the loyalty of various Asian groups, while employing its own racism against its neighbors. In addition, the growing cold war pitted the United States and the Soviet Union in a competition for the support of the mostly nonwhite Third World, while the Soviets began an effective propaganda campaign to show the dark-skinned peoples of Africa, Asia, and South America the hypocrisy of American racism. It quickly became clear after the war that if the United States was going to be a leader in a multiracial world, its racial policies in the South would have to change.

The credibility of racism was further undermined by a series of unusually heinous lynchings in the South; several were exservicemen, some still in uniform. These atrocities were reported graphically in the national press, and in nearly every instance the perpetrators were acquitted by a friendly local jury of whites. By 1947 these occurrences had brought an outcry from the North.

At the nation's universities new attitudes toward race began to emerge after the war, particularly in sociology courses where the social problem of America's race relations became a popular theme. Gunnar Myrdal's *An American Dilemma*, published in 1944, capped a series of important works that ripped away at the turn-of-the-century pseudo-scientific beliefs that had been the underpinning of white supremacy. (*See Document No. 1.*) In addition, public opinion polls showed that increasingly Americans believed that racism was a problem that the nation needed to confront in some way.

But at the same time, Americans were tired of conflict, weary of the battles against the Great Depression and the enemies of World War II. They were tired of experimentation and rapid change. The American people wanted stability and symmetry in their lives. They may have believed that civil rights for African Americans was inevitable, even advisable, but if such change came through conflict, or worst violence, they were not at all interested.

Americans may have wanted to avoid postwar crusades, but one emerged nevertheless, and it threatened to damage severely the civil rights movement. The Red Scare, the fear of the spread of world communism, consumed the nation in the postwar years, and unfortunately for blacks the civil rights movement was lumped together with all the other movements in America perceived as subversive. The civil rights movement was hardly radical in these early years, but the movement developed a radical image at least in part because several of its most prominent leaders, particularly Randolph, DuBois, and singer Paul Robeson, had declared themselves Marxists. This accusation of radicalism was further fueled by white supremacists who were prepared to grasp any opportunity to maintain the South's social and political structure; and they insisted that advocates of racial equality were soft on communism, and that there was a growing communist movement inside the black community. The tactic kept the civil rights movement at bay through the first half of the 1950s.

In response to such accusations and fears, civil rights leaders backed away from direct action as a method of protest, considering it much too radical for the times, and wanting desperately to avoid any hint of radicalism. With the exception of occasional successes by CORE in a few northern cities in the late 1940s, direct action ended until the mid-1950s.

That, however, did not mean that the civil rights movement hit a low point, only that it changed its tactics. The promise of direct action was replaced by the old standbys of litigation, legislation, and lobbying—the hallmarks of the NAACP. The association spent the next decade concentrating on fair housing, fair employment practices, voting rights, equal facilities for blacks, and the passage of federal antilynching and antipoll tax laws. Most of this work was invisible to the black masses, but little by little the NAACP chipped away at the walls of segregation and discrimination in the nation. For many black Americans the work of the NAACP was slow, inadequate, and delivered only symbolic victories. But in 1945 the NAACP was on the road to a major breakthrough that would change the movement—and America.

In the meantime, there were a whole series of subtle victories for the civil rights movement. In sports, desegregation was voluntary, and generally smooth. In 1946 Kenny Washington and Woody Strode signed with the Los Angeles Rams football team. A year later, in possibly the most important civil rights advancement outside the world of politics and the courts, Jackie Robinson joined the Brooklyn Dodgers and brought an end to segregated baseball in America. Robinson's great play on the field, and his sturdy character off, made him a source of pride for the black community, a true symbol of what the future of race relations in American might become.

At just the same moment, a symbol of southern racism was falling. In the 1946 midterm elections Theodore Bilbo was returned to his Senate seat from Mississippi. A staunch segregationist and white supremacist, Bilbo had won the election by intimidating black voters in Mississippi through such public statements as "You and I know what's the best way to keep a nigger from voting. You do it the night before the election. I don't have to tell you more than that." (*See Document No. 2.*) A Senate committee headed by Allen Ellender of Louisiana investigated the election and finally exonerated Bilbo of any wrong doing; but a bipartisan Senate committee refused to allow the Mississippi Senator to take his seat until it had time to review the case. While awaiting the Senate's decision, Bilbo died in August 1947. As Robinson symbolized the hopes and future of African Americans, Bilbo symbolized the age of Jim Crow, still ensconced in southern society, but clearly about to be challenged. Both men placed the race issue directly in the public eye.

The Election of 1948 and the Political Balance of Power.
The political arena in the postwar years still offered the best opportunity for African Americans to demand concessions from the federal government, and the presidential election of 1948 promised to be close. It would be an exceptional opportunity for blacks to follow up on the political successes of 1940. Harry Truman, the Democratic incumbent, had become president when FDR died in April 1945, and as polls showed at the beginning of the campaign season, he had not done particularly well. Historians would later exonerate Truman, but at the beginning of 1948 the American public did not agree. In fact, his lack of popularity took a toll on his party, which split wide open. At the beginning of 1948 Henry Wallace announced that he would run on a third party ticket and, he hoped, take a liberal-black–organized labor coalition with him.

By 1948 it was no secret that northern African Americans held the key to victory in a close presidential election, and that the coalition Wallace sought was potentially unbeatable. Truman made the requisite concessions to the liberals and labor in order to keep them in line, but the African American vote remained illusive, mostly because any concessions to civil rights brought a corresponding threat from the South to bolt the party.

Truman's advisors, however, soon concluded that to gain the northern black vote at the expense of the southern white vote might be a good trade. "A theory of many professional politicians," a Truman aide wrote the president in an important memo, "is that the northern Negro voter today holds the balance of power in Presidential elections [because black votes are] geographically concentrated in the pivotal, large and closely contested electoral states such as New York, Illinois, Pennsylvania, Ohio and Michigan." But what of the South? "As always," the memo continued, "the South can be considered safely Democratic. And in formulating national policy it can be safely ignored." This was a portent for the

future. In 1948 the Democratic party for the first time chose the northern black vote (the third side of the liberal-labor-black coalition) over
the southern white vote.

Truman responded to the advice, and to the northern outcry over the
lynchings in the South, by forming a committee on civil rights, and
promising to follow its recommendations. In October 1947 the committee published its report, *To Secure These Rights*, one of the milestones in
the history of the civil rights movement. (*See Document No. 3.*) *To Secure
These Rights* created an agenda that was much in advance of public opinion, and for the first time it brought the phrase "civil rights" into wide
usage. It blamed segregation for the problems blacks were having in
American society, and it placed the responsibility for solving those
problems squarely on the shoulders of the federal government. It called
for an end to the poll tax, an end to Jim Crow laws, and the desegregation of the armed forces. In February 1948, Truman incorporated many
of these recommendations into a civil rights message to Congress
and the nation. It set off a wave of hysteria in the South that led to the
Dixiecrat movement, and the nomination of Strom Thurmond for
president on a second third party ticket. Truman's message was the beginning of a major shift in the American political party system that
would not be played out until the 1960s when the majority of white
southerners would leave the Democratic party, and blacks (in the North
and the South) would vote Democratic in overwhelming numbers. It
was also the election that established civil rights as a key issue for the
future of American politics.

The day after the election, Truman told reporters that "labor did it."
But in fact, it was black voter strength that carried Truman over the top
in a number of key states, particularly California, Illinois, and Ohio.
Had any two of those three states gone to the Republicans, Truman
would have been left without a majority in the electoral college and the
election would have been thrown into the House of Representatives.

The election, however, did nothing to remove the power of southern
segregationists in Congress, and after the election they forged a powerful alliance with conservative Republicans to obstruct civil rights legislation. At the same time, Truman believed he needed to sacrifice domestic legislation for victories in foreign affairs. Consequently, several of
Truman's promises from the 1948 campaign were abandoned in order
to receive conservative support for his foreign policy agenda. Thus civil

rights in the late 1940s was often a sacrifice to the success of Truman's cold war initiatives.

The NAACP and the Court Fight Leading to the *Brown* Decision. In the immediate postwar years African Americans made significant gains in both the political arena and in the courts. Saddled with the stigma of being subversive at a time of anticommunist hysteria, the civil rights movement found few roads to travel beyond working within the system to bring change. It was the court battles, quietly fought by the NAACP, that finally brought on the breakthrough that would destroy Jim Crow and bring on the great changes of the following decade.

The NAACP continued its court crusade in the postwar period, a crusade that began its modern era in 1935 when the Supreme Court ruled in the case of *Grovey v. Townsend* that white primaries were not unconstitutional. It was a major defeat for the movement, and Charles Houston, the dean of Howard Law School, set out to change the situation by recruiting and educating talented black lawyers, men who could litigate before the Supreme Court where Houston believed the major battles against segregation and disenfranchisement ultimately would be fought. The result was Thurgood Marshall, a brilliant litigator and civil rights leader. Throughout his career, Marshall would argue thirty-two civil rights cases before the Supreme Court and win twenty-nine. In 1944, he succeeded in having *Grovey v. Townsend* overturned. It was his first major civil rights victory, and it was the beginning of a series of NAACP victories that would lead to the breakthrough decision of *Brown v. Board of Education* ten years later.

Such rulings slowly eroded the segregationist facade. But the biggest victories came in the court battles over segregated schools. As early as 1938 the court ordered, in *Gaines v. Missouri*, that an African American who had applied to the University of Missouri law school must be admitted since there was no other institution of equal status in the state. It was another twelve years before the court followed up on that judgement in two landmark decisions that led to the desegregation of over twenty southern universities by 1953, mostly at the graduate and professional levels. In *Sweatt v. Painter*, the court ruled that the hastily established blacks-only law school at Texas State University was not equal to the prestigious whites-only law school at the University of Texas.

Then in *McLaurin v. Oklahoma State Regents* the court said that a black student admitted to the University of Oklahoma Law School, but segregated from his white classmates, was not receiving an equal education under the law.

The NAACP's philosophy behind such cases was to force the southern states to produce the equal facilities for blacks demanded by the 1896 Supreme Court case of *Plessy v. Ferguson*. The intent was that the cost of segregation—the cost of maintaining two equal facilities—would become prohibitive and finally shake the South out of segregation. But that is not how the South responded. Seeing that their public school systems were becoming the target of the NAACP, southern school districts, in the early 1950s, went on a building spree in an attempt to provide separate and equal facilities for black students in order to avoid forced desegregation. By then, however, the question before the Supreme Court had changed. The court was no longer asking whether the separate facilities were of equal caliber, but whether schools separated by race could be equal at all. The NAACP had changed its philosophy. It now concluded that forcing the South to produce equal facilities for blacks did little more than to perpetuate the system of segregation. It would, instead, begin pushing for an end to segregation.

By 1950 Marshall and the NAACP were prepared to launch an attack on the South's segregated public school system. Their strategy was clear. They would argue that separation was fundamentally unequal. In May, the NAACP filed a suit in federal court in South Carolina asking that some sixty African American students be admitted to all-white schools in that state. Within the next two years four similar cases from Virginia, Delaware, the District of Columbia, and Kansas all reached the Supreme Court, all under the case title *Oliver Brown v. Board of Education of Topeka Kansas*.

The NAACP took on the case of Reverend Oliver Brown, pastor of Saint Marks African Methodist Episcopal Church in Topeka, who filed a suit against the city's board of education. Brown sought to overturn a Kansas state law that permitted cities to maintain segregated schools in the state. The law forced his nine-year-old daughter, Linda, to travel a long distance by bus to an all-black school even though she lived less than three blocks from an all-white elementary school.

In 1953, when Chief Justice Harlan Stone died suddenly, President Eisenhower named Earl Warren to head the high court. Stone had been a throwback to the old segregationist South and his death opened the door to a new liberal consensus on the court. Warren had been governor of California and the Republican vice-presidential candidate in 1948. He was considered an Eisenhower middle-roader, a political appointee, just another part of the Republican wave that was surging over Washington in the early 1950s. But Warren shifted the philosophy of the court immediately when it became clear that he was a strong believer in civil rights. Warren had allowed the internment of California's Japanese population during the war, and he may have sought some sort of atonement for his sins by pushing the court members to support desegregation. For whatever reason, Warren succeeded, and the court handed down a unanimous decision on May 17, 1954. (*See Document No. 4.*)

The question the judges asked themselves, and then answered, shows the change in the direction of the NAACP's arguments: "Does segregation of children in public schools solely on the basis of race, even though the physical facilities and other 'tangible' factors may be equal, deprive the children of the minority group of equal educational opportunities? We believe that it does." Then in conclusion, the court found "that in the field of public education the doctrine of 'separate but equal' has no place. Separate educational facilities are inherently unequal."

It was the most important civil rights breakthrough in the twentieth century. It overturned *Plessy v. Ferguson*, and set the movement on a path to the eventual destruction of legal segregation in the South. The resistance to it would, however, be strong.

CHAPTER 3

EARLY SUCCESSES AND
A HINT OF A SCHISM

The *Brown* decision was clearly a major victory for the civil rights movement. Many African Americans saw it as nothing less than a second emancipation, an intervention by the federal government on their behalf to end legal segregation in the South, much as the federal government had ended slavery some ninety years before.

Following the decision, the nation seemed to pause, waiting for the white South to respond, and it did not have long to wait. Georgia Governor Herman Talmadge predicted that any attempt to end segregation in the South would "create chaos not seen since Reconstruction," and, he added, "lead to the mongrelization of the races." Mississippi Senator James Eastland declared that "the South will not abide by nor obey this legislative decision by a political court." James Byrnes, governor of South Carolina, echoed his own dissent, insisting that the end of segregation in the South "would mark the beginning of the end of civilization in the South as we know it." But despite these almost requisite statements, the response from most of the South was not frothing racism or battle cries. Several major southern cities began moving toward the integration of their public school systems, and the general attitude was that such a decision from Washington was probably inevitable. There might be some local resistance, it seemed, and certainly some politicians would feel a need to shore up their political bases by complaining openly about the changes that were coming, but in most areas of the South it appeared that school desegregation would happen.

The *Brown* decision, however, was incomplete. In order for Warren to get the unanimous decision he believed was necessary to give credence to the decision, he apparently had been forced to compromise on several points to bring reluctant justices to his side. One result was that the original decision included no provisions, no details, no timetable for implementation—for the most part leaving it up to local school districts to carry out the law at their own discretion.

Despite the movements toward desegregation in the upper South, the NAACP had become frustrated that the Deep South was generally dragging its feet in desegregating its school systems. Thus a year after

Brown, the association began pushing the court to order instant and total desegregation. The court responded with what has been called the
"Second *Brown* Decision," requiring that school districts in the South
"admit [black students] to public schools on a racially nondiscrimina-
tory basis with all deliberate speed." The meaning of this proclamation
has divided historians. Was it a call to stop stalling and begin moving
forward on desegregation? Or was it a wink and a nod to the white South
that the court would not implement a specific timetable for desegregation—possibly the final price that Warren had to pay for his unanimous
decision. Whatever the answer, the result was that the South saw this
"Second *Brown* Decision" as an excuse to stonewall. The new strategy
for most of the thousands of southern school districts became to wait
until a federal court injunction forced each to desegregate. "All deliberate speed," it was clear, had no meaning.

The situation might have been different had the executive branch of
the federal government stepped in and enforced the court's decision.
But Eisenhower had no stomach for a battle against the forces of segregation. His inactions here clearly made the situation in the South far
worse than it otherwise might have been. Eisenhower often made private
statements in opposition to the *Brown* decision, but he never opposed it
in public. He believed, and said so often, that it was not his role to com-
ment on court decisions. At one point when asked during a news conference about the *Brown* decision, he responded only that "the Supreme
Court has spoken and I am sworn to uphold the constitutional process
in this country, and I will obey it." This deafening silence, however, allowed southern segregationists to claim that the president privately supported them, and that support from the executive branch justified their
actions. Eisenhower had an opportunity to provide the nation with
moral leadership on this issue, but he failed to do so, and that strengthened the segregationists' cause.

Eisenhower's silence, however, came more from his own belief in
gradualism than from his personal opposition to the civil rights movement. In fact, Eisenhower believed strongly that blacks in the South
should be given the vote, and that it was well within the proper sphere
of the federal government to guarantee that vote. Once given the vote,
Eisenhower believed, blacks would be able to remove the barriers of race
discrimination that had been erected against them over the centuries.
He also hoped that most of those black votes would fall onto the Republican side. To this end, Ike supported the Civil Rights Act of 1957

which, when finally passed after a two-year fight in Congress, emerged as essentially a voting rights bill. "With his right to vote assured," Eisenhower told a southern senator, "the Negro [can] use it to help secure his other rights."

First Actions and the Rise of Martin Luther King, Jr.

The history of the American civil rights movement often seems to begin abruptly with Rosa Parks's unwillingness to surrender her seat to a white bus patron in Montgomery, Alabama, in December 1955. But, in fact, the Montgomery Bus Boycott was the result of increased activity by the NAACP in the South since the end of the war, the result of a new black awareness nationwide, and a realization in the black communities that the archaic system of segregation could not stand against the forces of black unity—particularly if those forces were supported by the power of the federal government.

Everyday, some 40,000 African American bus riders—75 percent of the passengers—paid a dime to ride the Montgomery City Lines. Alabama state law required that the buses be segregated; the Montgomery city ordinance declared that the first five rows of each bus be designated for whites only. But once those rows filled, black riders had to move toward the back of the bus making more space for whites as they boarded the bus.

Blacks in Montgomery found this system intolerable. They complained regularly to the city commissioners, and in the spring of 1954, just after the *Brown* decision was handed down, black leaders threatened a boycott of the bus lines if the practice did not come to an end. By the beginning of 1955 an organization in Montgomery called the Women's Political Council (WPC) had developed a plan to boycott city buses. Led by college teacher, Jo Ann Gibson Robinson, the WPC believed that the boycott would be triggered by an incident, by one person's refusal to move to the back of the bus. Early that year a young black woman, Claudette Colvin, was dragged from a bus and arrested for refusing to give up her seat. Two NAACP activists in Montgomery, E. D. Nixon and Rosa Parks, began to raise money for Colvin's defense in federal court, but when it was found that Colvin was pregnant, they dropped their plans, fearing that the pregnant girl's credibility might be destroyed in the southern press. Two other similar incidents failed to provide what the plan needed, a figure of unimpeachable character.

It was Rosa Parks who provided that figure. Rosa Parks was forty-three years old, an activist in the local NAACP, a seamstress at a downtown Montgomery department store, and a participant in interracial workshops at the Highlander Folk School in Tennessee. On December 1 she boarded the Cleveland Avenue bus and sat in the fifth row, a portion of the bus open to blacks as long as whites were not left standing. When the whites-only seats filled, Parks and three other black riders were told by the driver to move back. The other black riders complied; Rosa Parks did not. The driver threatened to call the police. "You may do that," Parks responded. (*See Document No. 5.*) She was arrested and booked for violation of segregation laws. Later that evening she was bailed out of jail by E. D. Nixon and the movement had its cause.

By the next day, news of Parks's arrest had swept through the Montgomery black community, and the WPC decided to initiate its planned bus boycott in support of Parks. Although the initial planning of the boycott had come from the WPC, leadership quickly fell to the ministers of local black churches who immediately moved into the forefront of the movement by agreeing to preach the boycott in their church sermons on Sunday, December 4. The boycott, intended at first to last only one day, would begin the next morning.

On Monday evening, after one day's success, the city's black leaders called a meeting of the black community at the Holt Street Baptist Church. Several thousand attended, and quickly organized themselves into the Montgomery Improvement Association. After some haggling, the organization chose a president, the man who would lead the boycott that they now decided would continue. Their choice was a young minister, new to the town, Martin Luther King, Jr.

King, only twenty-six years old, had just completed a Ph.D. in theology at Boston University. His appointment as minister to the Dexter Avenue Baptist Church in Montgomery had come only fifteen months before the boycott began. But despite his youth and inexperience King was already well known throughout Montgomery's black community as an intelligent leader with powerful oratorical skills. It was King who would unite the African Americans of Montgomery into a powerful force for social change.

King had studied the nonviolent philosophy and practice of Mohandas Gandhi, and he believed (as did others at the time, including liberal theologan Reinhold Niebuhr) that nonviolent direct action might be a useful tool against segregation in the South—just as it had proven a useful tool against British colonial rule in Gandhi's India. But King's nonviolent philosophy did not reflect a radical faith. He would show over and over again through his career that he was a cautious leader, satisfied often with incremental progress and compromise.

By the end of December the boycott was becoming an economic issue. The Montgomery Bus Company, a private organization with its home offices in Chicago, was losing $2,000 per day. In addition, by early spring, a civic organization of local businessmen, calling themselves the Men of Montgomery, had begun to complain that the boycott was hurting downtown merchants. But the Montgomery White Citizens Council, an organization dedicated to maintaining segregation in Montgomery, pressed the city council to reject any compromise.

The members of the Montgomery black community remained united. They rode in car pools, and they walked ("protesting with their feet," as it was often described). They also used the several black-owned taxi services in the city, often paying a reduced fare, or none at all. The action attracted national media attention, as empty buses rolled across the nation's television screens.

In the end, victory came not because the city backed down, but because on November 13 the Supreme Court stepped in and upheld a federal district court ruling that the city's bus ordinance was unconstitutional. The decision became effective on December 20, 1956. The next morning, King, Reverend Ralph Abernathy, E. D. Nixon, and Rosa Parks boarded the first integrated city bus in Montgomery. Nonviolence had succeeded. Montgomery's black community had done little more than stop buying an unsatisfactory product. They had broken no laws (despite the city's attempts to find the boycotters somewhere in defiance of the law). It was a victory for nonviolence.

And the victory changed the face of the movement. Most importantly, King was catapulted into the role of the movement's primary leader, a position he would retain until his death. At the hands of the press, King received national attention. News reporters covered his speeches. Cameras followed him. In February when he was tried and convicted for violating an obscure Alabama antiboycott statute, the national press covered the trial. During the summer of 1956, King embarked on a nationwide speaking tour, bringing more attention to the boycott, and to himself. By the time the boycott ended in December, King was the national leader of the civil rights movement, chosen not only by blacks, but by white liberals as well—northern white liberals with money to give to the growing movement.

King understood the significance of the press. This was, in fact, possibly the greatest lesson learned from Montgomery. The press, particularly the northern press, was sympathetic to the movement, and a sympathetic press could sway a large northern constituency of wealthy liberals. Through King's leadership this alliance was forged early and it would fuel the movement into the mid-1960s. The key, of course, was to utilize—even manipulate—the press, and King quickly mastered the skill.

The Montgomery bus boycott became a rallying point for southern blacks. Unlike the *Brown* decision, which seemed to produce more rhetoric and good intentions than results, the boycott provided a tangible victory as a result of southern blacks banding together to force change. The boycott victory also placed the focus of the movement in the South and among southern blacks. Through most of the century the movement had been in the hands of civic leagues, like the National Urban League, and middle class legal aid societies like the NAACP. After Montgomery, leadership shifted to a broad network of independent churches that touched nearly every African American in the South.

Later the next year, the Southern Christian Leadership Conference (SCLC) was formed to coordinate black protest movements in the South. The founders were black ministers, and the philosophy was nonviolent direct action at the local level. The organization's base of operations was the southern black church where African Americans had traditionally congregated, prayed, held meetings, and socialized. Throughout the movement, local black churches in the South, under SCLC leadership, became the point of origin for hundreds of grassroots civil rights actions. They also served to coordinate and direct the greater movement as it spread throughout the South.

King was only one of several founders of the SCLC, but he quickly emerged as the organization's leader. His oratory skills, his national recognition, his brilliant victory in Montgomery, all served to thrust him into that role. It was also King's philosophy of nonviolence that became the philosophy of the SCLC. He realized that nonviolence could become a powerful and coercive instrument for social change. For the early civil rights movement King would be the leader, nonviolence would be the philosophy, and the SCLC and the southern black church would be the instruments of change.

Little Rock. By 1957 it was apparent that southern governors and other politicians in the South were winning elections by registering their defiance of the *Brown* decision, while moderates on race issues more often than not lost. The politics of race was nothing new in the South, but following the *Brown* decision it became increasingly clear that being on the wrong side of the race issue could end a political career. (*See Document No. 6.*)

In the late summer of 1957 Arkansas Governor Orval Faubus had come to believe that he faced a difficult fight for reelection to a third term. He had won the 1954 election on a platform calling for a progressive, modern Arkansas, but now in 1957 he felt the storm clouds of segregation and racism forming against him. He finally concluded that he had to campaign as a defender of white racism or lose the coming election. "If I don't do this," Faubus told Winthrop Rockefeller, the segregationists "will tear me to shreds."

Faubus got his chance to prove himself in the fall of 1957 when a federal judge demanded that the Little Rock school system begin the process of integration at once. On September 2, the day before the schools opened, Faubus announced that in order to maintain law and order he would use the Arkansas National Guard to stop the integration of Central High School in Little Rock. The next day, nine African American students approached Central High School and were turned away by National Guardsmen amid a crowd of several thousand jeering whites.

On September 20, a federal judge issued a court order demanding that Faubus remove the troops and proceed with integration "forthwith." Faubus complied with the order, but he replaced the troops with Arkansas State Police and continued to obstruct the registration of the nine students. On the next Monday, September 23, the nine students were allowed to enter the school. But when word spread among the white community that Central High School had been integrated, a mob began to assemble in front of the school. As the crowd grew in size and got uglier, the nine students were sent home. Nevertheless, violence erupted and whites rampaged through the city. Finally, the mayor of Little Rock sent an urgent message to President Eisenhower: "Situation out of control, and police cannot disperse the mob." Eisenhower responded the next day, September 24, by federalizing the Arkansas National Guard and sending in 1,000 paratroopers from the 101st Airborne Division. On September 25, the nine black students entered the school and the incident ended.

The events at Little Rock in the fall of 1957 merit study in the annals of the civil rights movement for several reasons. First, it was an important test of federal-versus-state power. It was, in fact, the first use of federal troops to protect the civil rights of blacks since the First Reconstruction; and it set the stage for the coming conflicts—conflicts in which federal authority would almost always win over the authority of the states. Second, it was the biggest test of the *Brown* decision. Faubus had stood in direct defiance of a federal court order seeking to enforce *Brown*—and he had lost the fight. The result was that *Brown* was strengthened significantly. Third, Eisenhower had done all he could to avoid intervening in the situation in Little Rock, and his inaction seemed to show that he did not support civil rights, or at least he would not intervene (unless absolutely necessary as in the case in Little Rock) to support the *Brown* decision. As a result of Eisenhower's inaction, segregation in the South slowed as other state governors insisted that they, too, would fight to stop integration. By the time Eisenhower left office three years after the confrontation at Little Rock, only 7 percent of black students in the South were enrolled in integrated schools.

Lastly, the incidents at Little Rock had a tremendous impact on the nation's attitude toward southern racism. They were covered heavily in the national press, both on television news and in the print media. For the first time many Americans could see the face of violence and hatred that was the segregated South. White Americans in the North had been told repeatedly through the twentieth century that the segregated system in the South was best for both blacks and whites; that blacks, in fact, favored the system. The press photos and films from Little Rock, however, made it abundantly clear that that was not true.

Among the nine blacks students was fifteen-year-old Elizabeth Eckford. A photograph of her wearing a white dress and being taunted by white students whose eyes and mouths spewed hatred and viciousness, hit the national press during the incident and was shown repeatedly on national television news. For many Americans in the North, Elizabeth Eckford was a victim, a sweet-looking little girl who wanted nothing more than to go to school and get an education. As King had learned in Montgomery, the media could be a powerful ally.

Sit-ins. Following the victory in Montgomery, the civil rights movement quieted for over three years. The reasons are difficult to find. Eisenhower's reluctance to enforce the *Brown* decision, and the corresponding power that southern segregationists seemed to gain as a result, may have stopped the movement in its tracks. For whatever the reason, the struggle was born anew on February 1, 1960. On that day Ezell Blair, David Richmond, Franklin McCain, and Joseph McNeil, four freshmen from the all-black North Carolina Agricultural and Technical College, sat down at a Woolworth's lunch counter in Greensboro and asked to be served. "The waitress looked at me as if I were from outer Space," one student later recalled. They remained seated and refused to leave. The next day they occupied the seats again, this time accompanied by twenty-five fellow students, and the next day by sixty-three students.

At first, news of the sit-ins spread through the southern black communities only by word of mouth. But the national press, eager to find something new in the long-quiet civil rights movement, quickly picked up the story, spreading the news and the movement like a wildfire throughout the South. Within two months there had been sit-ins in sixty cities in nine states involving thousands of young blacks who chose to defy the South's segregation laws en masse.

It was truly a grassroots movement. In fact, leadership and centralized coordination were nearly nonexistent. Young African Americans, often high school and college students, responded almost spontaneously by organizing, taking a seat, and closing down, at first, the segregated lunch counters, and then movie theaters, municipal swimming pools, public transit facilities, and even segregated public parks all over the South.

The NAACP, the SCLC, and CORE all tried to help the protesters (mostly working to get them released from jail), but it was not until the Student Nonviolent Coordination Committee (SNCC) was formed in April that the sit-ins became actively organized and planned. The idea for the SNCC developed from a need for a student arm of the SCLC, but at its organizational meeting in April the SNCC insisted on independence from the SCLC. Although willing to embrace King's nonviolent strategy, the SNCC was organized by young black activists whose philosophies tended toward a stance more militant than what King had in mind. In fact, the SNCC leadership often expressed dissatisfaction, even at this early date, with King's willingness to compromise and move cautiously. The SNCC soon attracted the most aggressive civil rights crusaders and would eventually become the focal point for the movement's most militant wing.

By the end of the year, some 70,000 people had taken part in the sit-ins in over one hundred southern cities and towns with the result that lunch counters in fifteen states had been desegregated. In some places the cost was high. Over 3,600 protesters were arrested; others were harassed or beaten as they sat in their seats. The movement was not always successful, and by no means did the sit-ins succeed in bringing an end to the segregation of public facilities in the South. But it instilled courage and confidence in those who participated, and it trained young black leaders and readied them for the major confrontations that lay ahead.

The sit-ins also marked the beginning of a commitment by John Kennedy to the civil rights movement, and that would have an important impact on the movement through the next decade. The 1960 presidential campaign began about the time the students sat down in Greensboro. Kennedy, who was nearly unknown in the black community, saw Eisenhower's lack of sympathy for black issues as a vulnerability to be exploited in his campaign against Vice President Richard Nixon. Against the advice of his more conservative advisors, Kennedy drafted a message for the demonstrators: "They have shown that the new way for Americans to stand up for their rights is to sit down." In late October, just days before the election, King was arrested at a sit-in demonstration in Atlanta and sentenced to a rural Georgia prison for four months. Again, Kennedy saw an opportunity to win black votes. He called King's wife, Coretta Scott King, to offer support. Robert Kennedy followed up by asking an Atlanta judge to expedite King's release, and King was immediately freed on bail. In a statement printed widely in the press, King's father, said: "It's time for all of us to take off our Nixon buttons." In the election, Kennedy took 68 percent of the black vote and won the election by a mere two-thirds of one percent of the popular vote. Black leaders came to believe that the Kennedy administration owed a political debt to the civil rights movement. At the same time, many whites would blame Kennedy for what they perceived to be the problems the movement caused.

The sit-ins also changed the movement dramatically, sending it down two divergent paths. One path was militant and led by the young, and increasingly more militant, leaders of the SNCC. The other path was moderate and guided by King and his church-based followers in the SCLC. Over the next three years the gap between the two philosophies would widen, and the movement would be irreparably damaged as a result.

Freedom Rides. The successes of the sit-ins inspired the freedom rides which began in early May 1962 just as the main thrust of the sit-ins were coming to an end. The rides were organized by CORE, which was at that time the most active of the several civil rights organizations. King's SCLC had done little to lead or organize since Montgomery, and the SNCC was still in its infancy. The NAACP continued on with legal defense and lobbying campaigns, and generally stayed clear of the direct action movement. It was CORE, almost by default, that had stepped forward to lead.

Two buses of riders left the nation's capital on May 4 and headed into the South. Roughly half the group were young African Americans and half older white pacifists and religious leaders. Their objective was to show that segregation continued in the South despite a 1947 Supreme Court ruling that outlawed segregated seating on buses, and a December 1960 ruling that ordered the desegregation of bus stations and terminals. Their plan was to take integrated buses into the South (with blacks sitting in the front and whites in the back) and at various stops along the way enter segregated bus terminals. "We felt we could count on the racists of the South to create a crisis so that the federal government would be compelled to enforce the law," James Farmer, CORE's new executive director, recalled. He was correct. As the buses continued into the Deep South the confrontations escalated. At Anniston, Alabama, one bus was fire-bombed, and in Birmingham there was a savage attack on the riders. The incidents received heavy coverage in the national press.

All this placed the new president in bad position, much the same position that FDR and Truman had faced through the 1940s. He was caught between the black voters who had supported him in the election, and the powerful southern Democrats who controlled Congress. As the freedom riders attracted more and more violence in the South, Kennedy was faced with supporting the riders and antagonizing southern congressmen, or turning his back on the riders to win the support of the southern leadership.

From Birmingham a new group of riders took the remaining bus on to Montgomery where a particularly vicious attack prompted the president to send in 600 federal marshals to protect the riders. On May 19, King arrived in Montgomery to lead the movement, and the next evening marshalls clashed with rioters who had trapped King and a large group of followers at Ralph Abernathy's First Baptist Church in Montgomery.

The second group of riders, most of whom were hospitalized, were forced to disband after the Montgomery attack. But on May 24, a third group announced that they would take the bus on to Jackson, Mississippi. Governor Ross Barnett agreed to use the Mississippi National Guard to protect the riders through the state. The plan worked, but when the riders reached Jackson they were arrested, charged with disturbing the peace, and sentenced to sixty days on a Mississippi state prison farm.

The freedom rides revealed a great deal about the civil rights movement, its leadership, and its relationship with the federal government. King, it was clear, was falling behind in the movement. At the height of tensions, Robert Kennedy had called for a "cooling off" period, a strategy that angered black radicals and made them question the sincerity of the Kennedy administration and white liberalism. King refused to accept the cooling off, but agreed to what he called a "lull." Again the radicals asked questions, but this time it was the sincerity of their own leader they doubted. Also, King was invited to travel with the third wave of freedom riders from Montgomery to Jackson. But citing his probation in Georgia, he demurred. He would not share the danger. "We came back from the freedom rides," one civil rights activist recalled, "with the terrible feeling that the angel had feet of clay." There was a clear rift developing between the more moderate-church-related groups led by King, and the younger radicals who were now rising to leadership in CORE and the SNCC. At this point the schism was of little consequence because the two groups needed each other. The radicals needed King's notoriety and the press coverage it attracted, while King needed the vigor and numbers that the young radical soldiers brought to the movement.

The freedom rides also reinforced the message to southern governors that there was great political capital to be made by campaigning against the civil rights movement, a legacy from Orval Faubus and the incidents at Little Rock four years before. The rides also revealed the dilemma that faced the new president. Black votes had been instrumental in his election only months before, but the Kennedys had balked at aiding civil rights, obviously in deference to powerful southern congressmen. King, seeing the importance of federal support, would continue to try and work with the administration. The radicals, on the other hand felt only disillusionment and disenchantment, and a need to make their own way without pandering to white liberals who they believed could only stifle their movement.

Early Signs of Two Divergent Paths. Following the freedom rides, Robert Kennedy concluded that such direct action could only damage the administration by forcing it to chose between black voters and the support of powerful southern congressmen. His solution was to try to direct black activism away from direct action and toward what the administration called "more constructive methods," particularly voter registration drives in the South. Such a plan, the administration reasoned, would avoid confrontation and violence while aiding the Democratic party since most new black voters would likely vote Democratic. In addition, not even the most extreme segregationist could oppose such a plan, and in the long run it might even serve to liberalize the conservative southern delegation in Congress.

At first, a number of radicals in the SNCC opposed this plan, insisting that the administration was trying to cool off the movement by forcing it into a more moderate stance. Others, however, saw the voter registration drive as an opportunity to organize at the grassroots level, and it was there, they argued, that the civil rights movement would have its most success. Thus the SNCC agreed to take the lead in organizing the voter registration drive. It sent full time, paid workers into the Deep South to register voters and work among poor blacks.

The voter registration drive changed the character of the SNCC. The workers in the Deep South were forced to confront the relationship between racism, abject poverty, ignorance, and the systematic destruction of the entire black culture. In addition, federal support for the voter drive was promised but never delivered, and the violence against the workers eventually eroded their faith in the philosophy of nonviolence as a response. What had been an organization made up of mostly middle class, urban college students, quickly became more radical.

It was King, however, who remained the movement's primary leader, chosen by blacks, certainly, but also by white Americans and their representatives in Washington. He was the least radical of the civil rights leaders, at the head of a movement that was bound to succeed. The Kennedy administration, and much of white America as well, was willing to allow the movement to go forward, but only under the leadership of a moderate like King. Consequently, it was King's activities that were supported by Washington with federal marshalls, with pressure on local judges to keep King and his followers from receiving long jail sentences, and in several cases with money channeled through wealthy white liberals. King also drew the white press. As these factors became more and more apparent to the growing radical elements inside the SNCC and CORE they began moving away from King and his SCLC.

This conflict between the two strategies in the movement reached a high point in Albany, Georgia in December 1961. The SNCC had organized the black community there to end the town's blatant segregation and, as they threatened, to "pack the jails for freedom." King came to town, got arrested twice, stole the spotlight from the SNCC, and then abandoned Albany without receiving any concessions. The *New York Herald-Tribune* called it a "stunning defeat." All of a sudden, King's headline-grabbing antics seemed more of a hindrance than an asset to the movement.

The movement was splitting, a schism was coming between the forces of moderation and the forces of a growing radicalism. And King saw it. His response was to move faster, be more confrontational, and to compromise less with federal authorities. The result would be a major encounter at Birmingham, the bastion of segregation in the American South. King knew if he could break Birmingham, segregation in the South would come to an end.

CHAPTER 4

THE ROAD FROM BIRMINGHAM TO SELMA

Birmingham. If the movement was on the verge of a major split it was not at all evident when King and his supporters took on the city of Birmingham in the spring of 1963. The Birmingham city government had made it clear several times that it would resist desegregation. But to King Birmingham was the key. He believed that if he could crack Birmingham the remainder of the South would fall to the forces of desegregation. "As Birmingham goes," he said, "so goes the South." Standing at the gates of Birmingham to do battle against King and the civil rights movement was Eugene "Bull" Conner, the city's long time police commissioner and enforcer of segregation. The forces were drawn up.

On April 12 King was arrested for defying a court order to stop demonstrating, and while in jail he wrote his *Letter from the Birmingham Jail*, primarily a scathing attack on white clergymen who had accused him of carrying the movement forward too quickly and too aggressively. (*See Document No. 7.*) To them, the assault on Birmingham was "untimely, unwise, unnecessary, and illegal." But King also warned of serious problems that might emerge within the civil rights movement if he did not receive support from white liberals. "I am convinced," he wrote, "that if your white brothers dismiss us as 'rabble rousers' and 'outside agitators'—those of us who are working through the channels of nonviolent direct action—and refuse to support our nonviolent efforts, millions of Negroes, out of frustration and despair, will seek solace and security in black nationalist ideologies, a development that will lead inevitably to a frightening racial nightmare." King clearly perceived the frustrations and impatience flowing from the young militants, and he saw what the future held if his movement for nonviolent change did not succeed.

King and others began leading marches and boycotts in the city during the first week of April, but the real showdown came a month later. On May 2 the black children of Birmingham began marching toward the city center. By the end of the day, the Birmingham police, using buses, had arrested nearly one thousand of the children. The next day, Conner escalated the situation by changing his strategy from arresting marchers to repulsing them. He then made the mistake that finally forced the administration in Washington to throw its entire weight behind the movement: Conner released police dogs on the marchers, many of whom were children. Others were clubbed and sprayed with seven hundred pounds of water pressure from the city's fire hoses. It was enough pressure, one marcher recalled, to remove the bark from trees.

That night, on national news reports, America watched in horror as snarling Dobermans ripped the clothes from peaceful demonstrators—who were asking for nothing more than equal protection under the nation's laws. The press had drawn the world's attention to Birmingham. The viciousness of the attacks, the shocking display of white racism, moved the nation. White Americans in the North were again shown that racial conflict in the South was a major social problem that would have to be solved. "The civil rights movement should thank God for Bull Conner," the president told an advisor privately. "He's helped it as much as Abraham Lincoln."

The violence escalated from marches to riots. Finally, on May 10, a downtown Birmingham group called the Senior Citizens Committee agreed to desegregate the city's lunch counters and hire black workers if King would call off the marches. King agreed. Conner and the segregationists fought back, insisting that those making the agreement did not represent the city. The next day the Gaston Hotel, where the movement had set up its headquarters, was firebombed. That same night a bomb destroyed the home of King's brother. The violence spread. Seven Birmingham stores were set ablaze. Kennedy sent 3,000 federal soldiers to Fort McClellan outside Birmingham in anticipation of federal intervention. The violence spread through the rest of the summer and fall, engulfing over 186 cities and towns throughout the South. Southern whites had lost the fight. They knew it, and they were venting their frustrations.

The Emergence of George Wallace. On June 11, Alabama Governor George Wallace kept his promise to "stand in the schoolhouse door" to prevent the desegregation of the University of Alabama. It seemed to be simply another incident of a southern governor making a symbolic statement in the name of segregation. One reporter wrote that Wallace would soon be "placed beside that old broken musketeer, Ross Barnett, in Dixie's wax museum." But Wallace's actions had more significance. The response to the speech was surprising, even to Wallace.

Through the following week the Alabama governor received over 100,000 congratulatory telegrams, and over half came from outside the South. For Wallace it was an epiphany: racism was not only a southern phenomenon. He began discussing with his advisors the possibility of a run for president the next year. The event at the schoolhouse door may have looked like just another southern governor's rantings, but it was, in fact, the beginnings of a major and debilitating backlash against the civil rights movement.

Wallace's speech was a short-term victory for the Kennedy administration. The president sent troops to Tuscaloosa, Wallace hid in the governor's mansion, and the university was integrated. That evening, Kennedy took the opportunity to address the nation. His impassioned speech marked an end to the administration's vacillation on civil rights and the beginning of five years of strong support from the White House for the civil rights movement. (*See Document No. 8.*) "We preach freedom around the world," Kennedy told America, "and we mean it, and we cherish it here at home, but are we to say to the world . . . that this is the land of the free except for the Negroes; that we have no second class citizens except for the Negroes, that we have no class or caste system, no ghettoes, no master race except with respect to Negroes?" He continued with another question: "[W]ho among us would be content to have the color of his skin changed and stand in [the Negro's] place? Who among us would then be content with the counsels of patience and delay?" America must "fulfill its promise," he added. "A great change is at hand, and our task, or obligation, is to make that revolution, that change, peaceful and constructive for all."

A week later the president proposed a bill that required the desegregation of public facilities, outlawed discrimination in employment and voting, and allowed the attorney general to initiate school desegregation suits. This would become the Civil Rights Act of 1964. Although most civil rights leaders wanted a stronger bill, it was the most far-reaching civil rights bill since the first Reconstruction.

The Movement's Pinnacle: The March on Washington.

By the late summer of 1963, the civil rights movement (as a nonviolent movement with the objective of ending legalized segregation in the South) was approaching success. There was enough energy left for a consolidation of victories, a celebration of an achievement: the March on Washington. It would be King's crowning glory.

The idea for a march on Washington had actually been conceived in 1941 by A. Philip Randolph. Here in 1963, at age seventy-three, Randolph hoped to bring the present civil rights movement together to mark the end of legal segregation in the South. It was also intended as a powerful message that African Americans and white liberals wanted the president's civil rights bill passed. The bill was then before Congress.

The Kennedy administration tried to persuade Randolph, Bayard Rustin and other leaders to call off the march, but as Randolph told Kennedy, "they'll come anyway." Realizing that it would be better to support the march than stand against it, the president decided to go along in hopes of moderating several planned antigovernment speeches. In one case, the administration's influence forced changes in a fiery antigovernment speech planned by the SNCC's John Lewis, much to the disgust of the movement's radical element that had, by then, come to distrust the Kennedy administration. The skirmish over Lewis' speech threatened to split the movement that was becoming increasingly fragile.

The march took place on August 28. Some 250,000 Americans, black and white, assembled peacefully on the Mall between the Lincoln Memorial and the Washington Monument. The high point of the day was King's "I have a dream" speech, the apex of his career as leader of the movement. (*See Document No. 9.*) King's strategies had succeeded.

Despite the efforts of the March on Washington, the Civil Rights Bill languished in Congress. It was Kennedy's death in November that finally shook the bill loose, and soon the bill came to represent a memorial to the slain president. The new president, Lyndon Johnson, threw his full weight behind the bill, and with the united forces of liberal lawmakers, civil rights leaders, organized labor, and various religious groups, an even stronger bill was finally passed, but only after the Senate shut down a filibuster of southern senators that had lasted for fifty-seven days. It was the first time the Senate had invoked cloture on civil rights, a signal that the Senate's once powerful southern bloc was in decline. The bill that was signed by Johnson, the Civil Rights Act of 1964, brought an end to legal segregation, and provided specific mechanisms to enforce the new law. Equal access become national policy.

The March on Washington, and the passage of the Civil Rights Act, did not bring an end to the civil rights movement. Those events were, however, a watershed that marked the coming of major changes and new objectives in the movement. It would now be directed toward removing prejudices and inequalities, with its focus directed toward legislative and political activity. The movement would also now concentrate, at least in part, on the inequalities in the nation's northern cities where the races were separated by a complicated social structure instead of local laws. And it would mark a change in leadership. Although King would certainly remain prominent until 1968, young leaders were beginning to move away from King's nonviolent protest philosophy; they were not in tune to the southern religious foundations of the movement, and they began to look toward new ideologies of black racial pride and black leadership, and away from an integrated movement. This new phase of the movement would be much more violent, and it would ultimately provoke a severe backlash. It would also be much less successful.

Freedom Summer. Many of these changes can be traced to the Freedom Summer of 1964, a biracial voting rights drive organized in Mississippi by the SNCC. The Freedom Summer had its origins in a mock election held the year before. It was a strategy designed to bring blacks into the polling place and have then cast votes as a way of protesting the mass disenfranchisement of Mississippi blacks. The SNCC also hoped that it would show that blacks wanted to vote, and that they indeed would vote. The strategy worked. Some 70,000 African Americans voted, and national media attention was averted for a while to the abomination of southern racism and a system that refused American citizens the basic right of the ballot.

The mock election was successful primarily because of some one hundred white students from Yale and Stanford universities who took two weeks off from school to work in Mississippi as volunteers for the SNCC. These students brought with them press coverage, increased FBI protection, financial and moral support from northern liberals, plus some exceptional organizing and leadership skills. The members of the SNCC, particularly Robert Parris Moses and Fannie Lou Hamer, were impressed by the volunteers' work, and they struck on the idea of sending out a general invitation to northern white college students to join the SNCC for the Freedom Summer of 1964, a planned voting rights drive throughout the South. Most SNCC leaders hoped the white students would bring increased press coverage to the movement. Others clearly believed that the action would bring on violence, and that if Americans saw the blood of white college students running in the streets of the South the pressure on the government to protect all civil rights workers would increase dramatically.

A vocal minority within the SNCC, however, saw the situation differently. They questioned the need for white workers as organizers in a black movement. Others believed that asking for white assistance somehow indicated an admission of black weakness, an inability to manage their own movement. Moses and Hamer continued to argue that white students would draw attention to the movement and increase federal protection for all the workers. Moses also argued that the movement should remain biracial. "Look," he told the members of the SNCC meeting in Greenville, Mississippi to discuss the issue, "I'm not gonna be a part of anything all black." Hamer agreed: "If we're trying to break down this barrier of segregation, we can't segregate ourselves." For the moment Moses and Hamer prevailed, and in February 1964 the SNCC sent out invitations to northern white college students to join in the Freedom Summer in Mississippi. Some nine hundred answered the call.

The SNCC trained and prepared the college students at Miami University in Oxford, Ohio, near Cincinnati. During the orientation word came that three civil rights workers had disappeared near Meridian, Mississippi. Missing were two white northerners, Michael Schwerner and Andrew Goodman along with a black southerner, James Chaney. President Johnson responded by sending FBI agents on an exhaustive search for the three workers and their murderers. The bodies were finally found, and twenty-one men near Philadelphia, Mississippi were charged with the murders. White blood had finally been spilled in the cause for civil rights.

Despite the murders, Johnson failed to protect the workers. Terrorists in Mississippi killed three other workers, assaulted eighty more, shot thirty, and burned some thirty-five churches in the state. Over one thousand civil rights workers were arrested. Soon they began to question the federal government's sincerity in aiding the movement or even in protecting the basic rights of civil rights workers, and many returned north in the fall disenchanted with the supposedly liberal White House and skeptical of the precepts of American justice. By the end of the Freedom Summer, most SNCC volunteers working in Mississippi had begun carrying guns.

The Mississippi summer project, however, was in many ways a success. Schools and community centers were set up throughout the state, and the nation focused its attention on the horrors of Mississippi racism and on the project itself for the entire summer.

Mississippi Freedom Democratic Party. The achievements of the Freedom Summer inspired the SNCC to turn its success and publicity into a political force. In that same summer of 1964 the Democrats were preparing to nominate Lyndon Johnson to a second term, and in Mississippi the state Democratic party had excluded blacks from the process of selecting delegates to the national convention. The members of the SNCC responded by forming the Mississippi Freedom Democratic Party (MFDP) and choosing their own delegates. They pledged their support for Johnson, and planned to attend the national convention in Atlantic City.

At the head of the MFDP delegation was Fannie Lou Hamer, a forty-one-year-old SNCC staff member. As part of the MFDP's plea for recognition, Mrs. Hamer spoke to the Democratic party credentials committee. She told of her poverty-stricken existence near Winona, Mississippi, and how she had tried desperately over the years to register to vote, to exercise her privilege as an American citizen. She explained that she was involuntarily sterilized, whipped, as she said, until her skin turned blue, and finally fired by her farm employer. It was an impassioned plea that was picked up by the press, and for a moment the plight of Fannie Lou Hamer caught the imagination of the American people—and threatened to turn the convention into a moral crusade for voter rights in the South. (*See Document No. 10.*)

Johnson, however, was determined not to allow that to happen. He was mired in the old Democratic party mud hole of having to satisfy northern liberals while trying to keep white southerners in line, and the appearance of the flamboyant Mrs. Hamer and the MFDP in Atlantic City threatened to disrupt this delicate balancing act. The members of the MFDP insisted, however, that they were the only legal representatives from Mississippi and that they should be seated as the only official Mississippi delegation. Throughout the convention Hamer and the other delegates continued to attract press coverage and that embarrassed Johnson.

To smooth the situation, Johnson sent Hubert Humphrey to forge a compromise that would satisfy both Mississippi delegations. With the hope of being chosen as Johnson's vice presidential candidate, Humphrey hammered out a compromise that gave the MFDP two "at-large" seats and allowed the remainder of the delegation to attend the convention as "guests." The members of the entire white Mississippi delegation were still allowed to cast all their votes for Johnson. The party promised that in the future it would draw up guidelines eliminating racial discrimination in the delegate selection process.

For the radicals inside the SNCC this was no compromise at all. It essentially removed the MFDP from the nominating process, while the all-white Mississippi delegation remained intact. The radicals were further disgusted that prominent white liberals like Walter Mondale, Wayne Morse, Walter Reuther, and even the MFDP's own Joseph Rauh, accepted the compromise. Even King and Bayard Rustin agreed to go along. In its final decision, the MFDP leadership refused to accept the administration's offer, choosing integrity over tokenism.

The result of the incident in Atlantic City was a further splitting of the movement between the moderate followers of King and the rapidly growing radical group inside the SNCC. For a growing number of young blacks, the liberal hopes represented by King and the white liberal establishment were quickly being replaced by a radical dogma that was feeding on disillusionment.

The 1964 election was a Johnson landslide, but it was not without its surprises. George Wallace had made an early run for the Democratic nomination and raised eyebrows when he grabbed an astounding 34 percent of the votes in the Wisconsin primary, 30 percent in Indiana, and 43 percent in Maryland before dropping out of the campaign. Wallace had come to realize something that other politicians in America had not yet realized, that working class whites in the North did not like the idea of equal rights for blacks. Wallace had found the backlash.

Selma and Voting Rights. Radicals inside the civil rights movement were becoming increasingly disillusioned with King and his moderates, but King still maintained his position as preeminent leader of the movement. And in 1965 he took his newly acquired status as Nobel Peace Prize winner to Selma, Alabama where he intended to show the nation that Alabama continued to deny blacks the right to vote. Selma was to be to voting rights what Birmingham had been to segregation just two years before. King chose Selma because only 335 of the 15,000 eligible black voters in Dallas County (where Selma was the county seat) were registered to vote. If there were a center for white resistance to the black ballot it was in Selma.

But again the radicals saw it all differently. A group of SNCC volunteers, led by the young radical Stokely Carmichael, had been mounting a grassroots voter registration drive in Dallas and Lowndes counties since 1963. They resented King's trespass on their territory, and they knew that his proposed march on Selma would give him the glory and the fund-raising potential that they believed they deserved.

King's voter-rights push in Alabama enjoyed the support of the federal government. Despite Johnson's landslide victory over Republican Barry Goldwater in the November election, the Democrats had lost five Deep South states where white conservatives dominated the polls and carried the states for Goldwater. At the same time, black voter turnout in those states had been light, under 40 percent. King and Johnson both believed that the removal of voting restrictions would bring more blacks to the polls and eventually place the Deep South again into the Democratic column.

In Selma, on January 2, King called for battle by announcing, "We are not asking, we are demanding the ballot." Two days later in his State of the Union address, Johnson promised to "eliminate every remaining obstacle to the right and opportunity to vote." On the opposite side of the battle line was Dallas County Sheriff James G. Clark, a man whose bigotry was only exceeded by Bull Conner. Clark, like Conner, had positioned himself before American television to do battle against far superior forces.

At first, Clark showed restraint by denying King the confrontation he wanted—and thus the press attention he needed—to carry out his campaign. Through most of January, King led dozens of peaceful daily marches to the Dallas County courthouse where blacks tried, mostly in vain, to register to vote. Then on February 1, Clark began arresting marchers—770 including King the first day, then 520 the next, and 330 the day after that. King was released on February 5 and immediately rushed to Washington to appeal to the president for voting rights legislation. Johnson agreed.

While King was in jail, Malcolm X arrived in Selma to speak to the marchers. Malcolm was invited by the SNCC, and his appearance was further evidence of the growing divisions between the SNCC and the SCLC. Malcolm had reached national stature as an outspoken militant Black Muslim minister, but he was also an ardent critic of King and his nonviolent strategy. The SCLC leaders feared that Malcolm's presence might escalate the situation and even wrestle the Selma campaign away from King's leadership, but Malcolm's message was restrained. In a speech at Brown Chapel in Selma, Malcolm said only that white America "should thank Dr. King for holding people in check, for there are other [black leaders] who do not believe in these [nonviolent] measures." Three weeks later Malcolm was murdered in Harlem. His impact on the movement, however, would be felt long after his death.

On February 18 black protester Jimmy Lee Jackson was shot to death and the Reverend James Reeb died of a beating in nearby Marion, Alabama. King planned a march from Selma to Montgomery for Sunday, March 8, to commemorate the deaths of Reeb and Jackson, and finally to confront Governor Wallace. But at the last minute King postponed the march, claiming he needed to be with his congregation in Atlanta. The march was rescheduled for Monday, and King left town.

But on Sunday morning some five hundred marchers gathered at Brown Chapel in Selma and prepared to march. King, by telephone from Atlanta, reluctantly gave his blessing to the marchers. Led by Hosea Williams of the SCLC and John Lewis of the SNCC, over six hundred marchers proceeded toward the Edmund Pettus Bridge and out of Selma toward Montgomery. Without warning, at the far end of the bridge, some five hundred Alabama state police fell on the marchers and crushed them with clubs, chains, C-4 tear gas, whips, and electric cattle prods. In fear for their lives, the marchers turned and fled back toward the city only to be met by Jim Clark's advancing forces who had been given orders only "to get those god-damned niggers." Bloody Sunday was a brutal display of raw aggression that was seen by forty-eight million television viewers across the nation. King had wanted a Birmingham-like confrontation at Selma to force Johnson's hand on voting rights legislation. Although he was absent from the event, he got what he wanted at the Pettus Bridge.

King then announced that he would lead the marchers on to Montgomery on Tuesday March 9, but a federal court order against the march caused him to balk. As tensions mounted, President Johnson, fearing a bloodbath, asked King to call off the march, and he sent an emissary to Selma to negotiate a compromise between King and the police. On Tuesday morning, fifteen hundred marchers arrived from all over the country and prepared to defy the court order and march to Montgomery. King knew that if he did not march he risked alienating those in the movement who saw him as a compromiser. But if he did march he might alienate Johnson, who had just begun pushing for voting rights legislation. Despite his premarch words that "I would rather die on the highways of Alabama than make a butchery of my conscience," King relented. He led the marchers to the Pettus Bridge where the Alabama state police had again drawn up. He asked the marchers to kneel, pray, and return to Selma.

It is generally agreed that King's decision at the Pettus Bridge on March 9 was the correct one. It avoided the possibility of another attack on the marchers, and it kept the support of the Johnson administration. But it also further alienated the radical elements in the SNCC; they continued to question King's leadership.

On March 13, President Johnson, during a press conference (with an admonished George Wallace at his side) called the incident at the Pettus Bridge "an American tragedy," and then announced that he was sending a voting rights bill to Congress. Two days later, in a televised address to a joint session of Congress, the president committed his administration to voter rights in the South. (*See Document No. 11.*) It was his finest hour. "Should we defeat every enemy," he told America, "and should we double our wealth and conquer the stars, and still be unequal to this issue, then we will have failed as a people and a nation." He went on to ask Congress for a bill that would "establish a simple uniform standard which cannot be used, however ingenious the effort, to flout the Constitution. . . . Every American citizen," he added, "must have an equal right to vote. There is no reason which can excuse the denial of that right. . . . This cause must be our cause too. It is not just Negroes, but all of us, who must overcome the crippling legacy of bigotry and injustice. And," he added, "we *shall* overcome." The statement had behind it the full weight of the administration without compromise or deference to southern congressmen.

The administration's voting rights bill called for an end to literacy tests as a method of denying voter rights; and it authorized the attorney general to send federal registrars to states and counties where patterns of voter exclusion were apparent. Johnson was on solid political footing; Gallup reported that a convincing 76 percent of the nation favored the bill. The president exerted firm leadership in guiding the bill through Congress, where it met little resistance even from southern congressmen whose racist stance was becoming less and less tenable.

On March 21, 1965 the march from Selma to Montgomery finally proceeded under the protection of 3,000 federalized Alabama national guardsmen. Five days later, the marchers entered the state capital some

30,000 strong in a triumphant procession. The prominent and well-known joined in the last day's march. Rabbis, priests and ministers, entertainers, political figures, celebrities all joined, assuring massive media coverage. King spoke eloquently of the Promised Land and of going forward together. But the movement was badly divided, and the Promised Land was still very far away.

CHAPTER 5

BLACK POWER AND BACKLASH

The Rise of Black Power. The growing problem within the civil rights movement was more than just rebellious youth, more than a few hotheaded kids who wanted to lead with more flamboyance and dynamism than King. It was, in fact, a completely different approach, and a total rejection of King's philosophy of nonviolence. King's chief critic was Stokely Carmichael, a young, charismatic SNCC organizer. Carmichael, like others in the SNCC, disliked pinning the fortunes of the civil rights movement on one charismatic leader like King. Such dependence, Carmichael argued, robbed strength from local leaders. Carmichael had opposed the Mississippi Freedom Summer project in 1964, and instead headed off to organize a voter rights drive in Alabama. He opposed the MFDP, and considered the compromise a liberal hypocrisy. He resented white interference in what he believed should be an all-black movement, and he argued that African Americans needed their own political party that could function outside the existing all-white party system. In May 1966, Carmichael, at age twenty-four, defeated John Lewis as chairman of the SNCC and began pushing the organization further away from King's philosophy. At Carmichael's direction, white volunteers were expelled from the SNCC and the organization issued a statement calling for "black Americans to begin building independent political, economic, and cultural institutions that they will control and use as instruments of social change in this country." In January the SNCC declared its opposition to the war in Vietnam and offered sympathy to draft resisters. CORE was experiencing nearly a parallel transformation. Led first by black power advocate Floyd McKissick and then by the more radical black separatist Roy Innis, CORE formally reputed nonviolence in 1966, denounced the Vietnam War, and endorsed black power.

Black power as a slogan had its birth just weeks after Carmichael was elected chairman of the SNCC. In early June 1966, James Meredith, who had gained notoriety for having integrated the University of Mississippi four years before, set out on a march through Mississippi to show that blacks there were not free. On June 6 he was shot and wounded. King decided to pick up Meredith's personal march, and he was joined by Carmichael of the SNCC, Floyd McKissick of CORE, and several hundred marchers. These three men, at the head of the march, continued on to Jackson, arguing their philosophies along the way, with McKissick holding the middle ground somewhere between Carmichael and King.

At Greenwood, on the eleventh day of the march, Carmichael (after having just been released from jail) yelled to a crowd that had assembled outside the courthouse, "I ain't goin' to jail no more! I ain't goin' to jail no more!" The crowd began to chant "freedom now," the authorized slogan of the march. Carmichael's friend, Willie Ricks, began to shout "black power!" The crowd picked it up. Carmichael began directing the chant from the courthouse steps, and quickly "black power" drowned out "freedom now." The next day, King objected to the slogan. "We must never seek power exclusively for the Negro," he insisted, "but the sharing of power with the white people." The new phrase, he said, "would confuse our allies, isolate the Negro community, and give many prejudiced whites, who might otherwise be ashamed of the anti-Negro feeling, a ready excuse for self-justification." The press, looking for something new in the now stale story of civil rights, found what it was looking for in black power, and quickly black power hit the nation's headlines.

For many black Americans—particularly young black Americans—compromise, gradualism, and a satisfaction with overcoming racism and discrimination someday in the future was simply not enough. They had also come to believe that relying on white liberals, in fact relying on whites at all, had time and again damaged the civil rights movement—held it back by injecting a need to compromise with the white leadership. And for many blacks King was the problem. He was the black leader chosen by whites to lead the movement, a moderate who believed in nonviolence, who would compromise with the white leadership, and who continually accepted the empty promises flowing from Washington. What King had come to represent, in the minds of these young radicals, was failed liberalism, the promises and hopes for change that were only a blatant lie. The so-called great achievements of the civil rights movement, the Civil Rights Act and the Voting Rights Act, were nothing more than a conferring on African Americans the rights that had long been guaranteed by the Constitution and denied blacks by whites through illegal means. Clearly, the political system could go no further toward racial equality, and King's Promised Land seemed a long way off. The only alternative, these radicals had come to believe, was black nationalism, a closing of ranks, a total reliance by blacks on blacks. Carmichael believed that African Americans must maintain their own identity, their own community institutions, and their own movement free of white interference.

Carmichael had based his black nationalism on the ideas of Malcolm X. By the time Carmichael had risen to prominence as head of the SNCC, Malcolm was dead, assassinated in the early months of 1965 by his Nation of Islam enemies. He had, however, touched Carmichael and many other young African Americans living in the northern ghettoes, principally through his *Autobiography of Malcolm X* which swept black America after his death. Malcolm called for black pride, pride in black African roots, and pride in the ability of blacks to control their own destiny. He called for a "revolt of the American Negro" as part of "a global rebellion of the oppressed against the oppressor, the exploited against the exploiter." He often mocked King, his nonviolent philosophy, and his "I-have-a-dream speeches." By the time Malcolm had died, his militant stance had awakened thousands of poor and oppressed African Americans to his message of black nationalism.

Black power had a great impact on the civil rights movement, but it never really developed into a completely coherent ideology. In fact, the very definition of the term divided black America in the mid-1960s. Carmichael tried several times, through books and articles, to define the concept, but the term seemed to find its way into every corner of the movement. Moderates often used the phrase to describe race pride. Radicals saw it as a call to separatism, while still others saw it as an anticapitalist, anti-American, or even an antiwar slogan. For many African Americans black power was expressed simply in hair styles and a certain dress code, speech patterns, and even in the soul music of James Brown and other black performers who called for race pride. (*See Document No. 12.*)

Black power was denounced immediately, however, from the white liberal establishment and from the black leaders of nonviolent protest in the nation. King called it "negative," lacking the "substance and program to become the basic strategy for the civil rights movement." Black power was a gratifying slogan, he admitted, but it was nothing more than a "nihilistic philosophy born out of the conviction that the Negro can't win." Roy Wilkins of the NAACP said of black power, "We of the NAACP will have none of this. We have fought it too long. It is the

ranging of race against race on the irrelevant basis of skin color. It is
the father of hatred and the mother of violence." (*See Document No. 13.*)
White liberals denounced it. President Johnson condemned it, as did
Robert Kennedy, who by 1966 and 1967 was quickly emerging as the
leader of the Democratic party's liberal wing. Bayard Rustin became
the chief African American spokesman in opposition to black power,
calling its leaders "racist demagogues." It was to many observers, however, also the logical progression of the movement, a venting of anger
and frustration over unfulfilled promises and a policy of slow-moving
gradualism.

The black power movement had a further impact. It pushed white
liberals out of the civil rights movement. As the SNCC became more
and more militant, the once-ample funds from white liberals dried up.
Carmichael moved away from the SNCC and toward the Black Panthers, possibly the most radical of the black separatist organizations; and
his successor as chairman of the SNCC, H. Rap Brown, quickly made
Carmichael sound like a moderate with his frequent calls to "burn, baby,
burn!" By the end of the sixties, the SNCC, the primary leader of the
civil rights movement in the South, was bankrupt and effectively dead.
CORE quickly followed.

Frustrations and Riots. Malcolm's philosophy had its greatest
impact in the northern urban ghettoes where African Americans were
not denied the use of public accommodations and where they had the
right to vote, but where racial discrimination remained strong, systematic, and often as demeaning and violent as in the South. Ghetto housing was deplorable, city services such as police protection and education
were usually inadequate, and job discrimination left most blacks at the
bottom of the social and economic structure. At the same time, these
northern urban blacks had, like all Americans, grasped on to the hopes
and promises of the postwar era, the promises to end poverty, establish
equality, and bring peace and prosperity to the greatest nation on earth.
But the promises had been empty and often politically motivated.

Blacks had seen some improvement. African American family median
income had increased from about $6,000 in 1964 to $8,000 by the end
of the decade, and unemployment had dropped from 7.2 percent to 2.5
percent between 1962 and 1970. But the quality of life in the ghetto had
not improved. In fact, during the sixties ghetto life had deteriorated significantly; and in a telling statistic, nonwhite youth unemployment had

increased from 24 percent to 30 percent during the decade. At the same time, the civil rights movement in the South had stimulated rising black expectations, but the pace of that movement was slow and the movement's goals of ending *de jure* segregation and disfranchisement had little to do with the problems blacks faced in the northern cities. Black power, rather than civil rights, grew to become the creed in the ghettoes. And between 1965 and 1970 urban riots, rather than marches and sit-ins, became the chief method of protest.

Riots first broke out in Harlem in the summer of 1964, and then in Rochester, Jersey City, and Philadelphia later that same year. Americans barely noticed. But a year later, Watts, a sprawling black ghetto in central Los Angeles, erupted into a spectacular six-day riot that left thirty-four dead, over 1,000 injured, and $40 million in property damage. It took 14,000 National Guardsmen and 1,500 law enforcement officers to quell the riot. It was the end of the nonviolent movement in America. (*See Document No. 14.*)

Watts broke out just five days after President Johnson signed the Voting Rights Bill, and the president, not unlike most of the nation, was astonished by the events. While America watched Watts burn, another riot broke out in Chicago. The movement was changing dramatically. At the beginning of the year, King had moved to Chicago in what seemed to be an attempt to get out in front of the movement's new direction. But his philosophy of nonviolence fell mostly on deaf ears in the northern ghettoes.

The next summer brought on riots around the country in most major cities. National Guard troops patrolled the streets of Chicago, Milwaukee, San Francisco, Cleveland, and Dayton. Through the remainder of the decade massive riots swept across the nation. Almost every American city in the Northeast, Midwest, and California experienced a racial upheaval. The situation was unparalleled in the nation's history. The tally was 250 deaths, 10,000 injuries, and 60,000 arrests. Watts was the first major riot, but the 1967 six-day-long Detroit riot was the largest and most destructive. Fifteen thousand Michigan state police and National Guardsmen were ordered into Detroit to put down the riot that took forty-three lives and injured another 2,000. The loss of property was finally placed at $250,000. The target in Detroit, as in most other urban riots of the sixties, was white-owned businesses. Nearly 3,000 white-owned businesses in the ghetto were looted during the Detroit riot, and half of those were burned down or destroyed. Fourteen square miles of Detroit's inner city burned, leaving over 5,000 African Americans homeless. Detroit's mayor compared the carnage to postwar Berlin.

Other riots in that "long hot summer" of 1967 destroyed large sections of Newark, Boston, Cincinnati, Providence, New Haven, and Buffalo. Even small towns did not escape riots, particularly small towns in the industrial Midwest and Northeast with proportionally large black populations.

White Americans were dumbfounded by the riots. As they watched the chaos on their televisions they asked why blacks would resort to burning their own neighborhoods, local businesses, even their own homes? The answers, at first, came in studies. The McCone Commission, headed by former CIA Chief John McCone, explained away the Watts riot as the work of a few alienated black youths. Other analyses insisted that most African Americans deplored the riots and were satisfied with the gradual liberal reforms emanating from Washington. President Johnson, however, was not satisfied with the analyses, and in July 1967, while Detroit burned, he appointed Illinois Governor Otto Kerner to head a commission to study the riots. The Kerner Commission, in its *Report of the National Advisory Commission on Civil Disorders*, reported that "white racism is essentially responsible for the explosive mixture which has been accumulating in our cities since the end of World War II." (*See Document No. 15.*) In its final analysis, the commission, in its most telling response, noted that the nation is "moving toward two societies, one black, one white—separate and unequal." Urban blacks were simply making no significant gains. *En masse* they were involved in the riots, alienated, angry, militant, demanding changes in an American system that relegated them to a lower place in the economic order simply because of their skin color. They had been promised first-class citizenship. They had been promised a shot at the American dream by the liberal politicians in exchange for their votes. But the promises had gone unfulfilled.

By the late 1960s black power had entered the American vernacular, and at least in the minds of most of the nation, civil rights had gone from a movement for social change to a movement of demands and violence to force change. Television images of burning cities, firemen being shot at, gun-wielding Black Panther "soldiers," and the antiwhite tirades of Carmichael, Brown, Eldridge Cleaver, and Bobby Seale drove white America (whether once sympathetic to civil rights or not) away from the movement. White Americans were frightened by the militant rhetoric: "You'd better get some guns," Rap Brown told a crowd in Cambridge, Maryland. "The man's moving to kill you. The only thing the honky respects is force. . . . I mean, don't be trying to love that honky to death. Shoot him to death, brother, cause that's what he's out to do to you." (*See Document No. 16.*) Whites called for law and order in the streets instead of sympathy for protesters, punishment instead of understanding. At the behest of white voters, money was withdrawn from government-sponsored antipoverty projects. Congress refused to pass additional legislation to help the inner cities, inner city schools were left to decay, and ultimately whites fled to the suburbs, leaving the decaying inner cities to a growing black underclass.

Backlash. The white response to much of this was a severe and debilitating backlash that destroyed many of the gains of the civil rights movement. This white backlash was not only in response to the civil rights movement or calls for black power. It was a broad backlash against what is often called the excesses of the sixties. Race, however, played a significant role in the backlash. And although the backlash is discernable as early as 1964, it picked up considerable steam the moment "black power" replaced "freedom now" as the call of the civil rights movement.

In 1963, when Lyndon Johnson became president, only 31 percent of those asked felt that the federal government was pushing integration too fast. Within five years that number had jumped to more than 50 percent. What had happened? What had caused such a change?

In 1964 George Wallace ran for the Democratic nomination and took a surprising number of votes in three northern and border states before dropping out of the campaign. His successes showed clearly that a backlash was growing, not just in the South, but in the North as well, particularly among the northern working classes who despised civil rights agitators (along with antiwar demonstrators). Much of this had to do with a growing fear in the North that blacks were moving outside the ghettoes and into white schools and white neighborhoods, often into white working-class neighborhoods that frequently bordered black ghettoes.

In 1964 Wallace handed over the newly exposed backlash to the Republican candidate Barry Goldwater who went down to a ignominious defeat under the Johnson steamroller. But Wallace surfaced again in the

1968 campaign, this time running as an independent. In the general election he pulled the racist votes in the South, and again he showed surprising strength in the North among the white working classes. He almost never raised the issue of race specifically, but he railed against "forced busing," and "lawless street punks and demonstrators." He warned of the dangers posed by civil rights agitators and antiwar activists who mocked American and traditional Christian values. He accused federal officials of threatening the property rights of homeowning Americans, and federal judges of protecting the criminal and penalizing the victim in their obsession to protect civil liberties.

That summer Wallace drew 70,000 supporters at a rally in Boston, 15,000 in Pittsburgh, 12,000 in San Francisco, and 15,000 in Detroit. In October he climaxed his presidential race by packing Madison Square Garden in New York, the very heart of American liberalism. He told the crowd: "We don't have riots in Alabama. They start a riot down there, first of 'em to pick up a brick gets a bullet in the brain. That's all." The crowd erupted. The alienated Americans had found their champion.

As the campaign progressed, polls showed that Wallace would have an impact on the election by taking most of the South, but it was also clear that he would take votes from the Republican candidate Richard Nixon in several other key industrial states in the Midwest. Although Wallace would not win those states, desertions from the Republican party to Wallace could give several states to Hubert Humphrey, the Democratic candidate.

By September Nixon came to realize that he would have to shore up his southern base or risk losing the election. His response was to undercut Wallace's racism. In an interview in Charlotte, Nixon attacked mandated school desegregation plans and court ordered busing, calling both "counterproductive." Nixon eked out a narrow victory by only 1 percent of the popular vote. Wallace took the Deep South, but Nixon probably lost no states to Humphrey because of Wallace's impact.

Nixon had learned the lesson well. He began planning immediately for his reelection in 1972, and he would work to maintain his base of support in the South and among those conservatives outside the region who had rallied to George Wallace. He called this group the "Silent Majority," those white working-class and middle-class Americans who were determined to regain control of a society they felt had run amok in permissiveness and special privilege. Nixon's backlash was broader than the issue of race, but race was certainly the glue that held together his "silent majority" strategy. Nixon spoke often of containing welfare costs, of his opposition to court ordered busing, quotas, and affirmative action.

The Dream and the Death of the Dreamer.

In 1967 King came out against the war in Vietnam. As a man of peace and nonviolence he believed he could do nothing else. He had begun to see the war as heinous, a conflict ten thousand miles away, robbing the nation of the resources it needed to create new jobs and eradicate the nation's slums. The decision, however, hurt his place in the movement. President Johnson responded by doing all he could to destroy King's influence. Moderate black leaders like Bayard Rustin, Roy Wilkins, Andrew Young, Ralph Bunche, and Jackie Robinson criticized King openly. As violence in the streets intensified, and the white backlash took root, King seemed to fall from grace. In an attempt to get the movement back on track, he began planning for a Poor People's March on Washington, a multiracial action that, King hoped, would draw the movement's focus away from black nationalism and those who wanted an all-black movement.

In March, he went to Memphis to support a strike of the mostly black sanitation workers there. The march he led erupted into a riot as black youths went on a rampage and began looting the downtown district. It was a clear indication of how King's place in the movement was rapidly eroding. Nevertheless, King promised to stay in Memphis, insisting that he would show that a peaceful march was possible.

On April 3, in what has been called prophecy, King told a crowd "I've seen the promised land. I may not get there with you, but I want you to know tonight that we as a people will get to the promised land." The next night, while standing on balcony of a Memphis hotel, King was murdered by a white assassin.

Immediately, riots broke out in over a hundred cities. First Chicago, then Washington. Forty-six died and three thousand were injured throughout the country. Heavily armed troops guarded the White House and Capitol grounds. In Vietnam race riots broke out at American military bases.

The question was immediate: had the dream died with the death of the dreamer? King had held the center of the movement, its real strength. He had maintained its integrated nature that gave it power, money, and the support of the federal government. And clearly he had been the movement's inspiration. Yet in many ways it was already dead. The movement had begun to defuse as early as Selma, even possibly as early as Albany, but after 1965 it had been disintegrating rapidly. Even the incidents at Memphis, where King's peaceful march deteriorated into an urban riot, indicates the direction the movement was headed— and how it had all slipped from King's grasp. After King's death there was no longer a center to hold. Leaderless, the movement headed off into different directions, divided and weak.

Following King's death, Ralph Abernathy tried to keep the movement's momentum going by leading the King-inspired Poor People's March. Participation at the march was sparse. The SCLC leaders were arrested, and the crowds of poor were dispersed by police. Few noticed. Abernathy, who had been at King's side since Montgomery, was soon overshadowed in the SCLC by the flamboyance of Jesse Jackson. In 1971, Jackson split the movement further by forming his own Operation PUSH.

By 1972 the backlash had become ingrained. In that year Wallace made a third run for the presidency, this time running as a Democrat. In the primary campaign he took Florida with a surprising 42 percent of the vote, then Tennessee and North Carolina. And again he showed strength outside the South, finishing first in Michigan then in Maryland, and pulling strong second-place finishes in Wisconsin, Pennsylvania, and Indiana. In Maryland, in mid-May, Wallace was shot. The bullet paralyzed him for life, and he left the campaign. In a shift that would be a portent for the future, the backlash, then firmly in Wallace's grasp, slipped into the Republican party which would, from then on, be the harbinger of the backlash movement.

This backlash, now in the hands of Nixon and the Republicans, was not only a backlash against the successes of the civil rights movement. Nixon took on all the excesses of the sixties, from student demonstrations to drug use and permissive sex. But clearly, race led the way, and Nixon realized it. He opposed busing by calling for a moratorium on any additional court ordered busing until mid-1973. He said he would "end segregation in a way that does not result in more busing." In his 1972 campaign he promised to contain welfare costs, and curtail affirmative action and quotas. Nixon won the election, and he took the entire South. Blacks gave the losing candidate, George McGovern, over 85 percent of their votes.

CHAPTER 6

THE MOVEMENT IN ITS POSTREFORM ERA

Two Paths. In the postreform era of the civil rights movement black Americans headed off into two distinct directions. One group found solace in black nationalism through which rioting became the chief form of protest. Another group took up the ballot as a primary means of being heard, hoping to build on the legal rights it had acquired during the protest movements. Robert Kennedy had wanted this, so had Lyndon Johnson. It reflected the traditional liberal view that the remedy to all social and economic problems rested with the ballot.

In fact, if anyone took up the leadership of the movement's moderates after King's death, it was the black political leaders; not messiahs, but leaders who had the power to advance the interests of the black communities they represented. Carl Stokes was elected mayor of Cleveland in 1967. That same year, Richard Hatcher became mayor of Gary, Indiana. In 1973, Coleman Young was elected mayor of Detroit, Maynard Jackson was elected in Atlanta, and Tom Bradley became the mayor of Los Angeles. Between 1967 and 1977 there were black mayors elected in Newark, Washington, Oakland, Birmingham, and New Orleans. In each case, these elected leaders found a need to build coalitions with the white electorate to win elections, and to compromise, as all politicians must do. Thus they tempered the movement; they were less radical. They were themselves from the black middle class, and, more than any other, they represented that group.

Almost always these black politicians delivered to their constituency. The result was that black communities received better garbage collection, more paved streets, increased recreation facilities; and, of course, blacks received more and better jobs. But these politicians inherited big problems, including the consequences of a weak national economy through the 1970s, increasingly dwindling federal funds, and white flight to the suburbs, which left behind an increasingly poor population and a severely weakened urban tax base.

These leaders, out of political necessity, represented a multiracial group of voters, but inside the African American community they clearly represented an emerging black middle class. These middle-class blacks were often well educated. They voted, and their influence was strong, particularly on the local level. This group had succeeded by working within the white-dominated society and accepting its values and its limitations. In 1960 only 13 percent of the black population could count themselves as middle class. By the late 1970s, however, that number had jumped to over one-in-three. For this group the civil rights movement had been a rousing success. They had been patient, and they had reaped the rewards of the movement.

A large portion of the black population, however, continued to live in poverty. In 1980, that number had increased to over 30 percent, almost four times that of whites; and the unemployment levels of young black males reached depression-era levels at an astronomical 40 percent. In addition, 40 percent of black children lived in single parent households, and half of those were in poverty.

The Political Arena. In the national political arena, African Americans became a major force in the 1970s, and they found their place in the Democratic party. At the Democratic National Convention in the summer of 1976 over 10 percent of the delegates were black, and it was the Mississippi delegation that had the highest percentage of black delegates. At that convention the Democrats nominated Jimmy Carter, and in the general election blacks gave him 90 percent of their votes in the closest election since 1916.

The most important question involving black Americans during the Carter years was affirmative action. In a 1972 survey, 82 percent of whites opposed affirmative action and quotas. They considered such plans to be preferential treatment in hiring and college admissions practices—in fact, reverse discrimination. Blacks, on the other hand, argued that as long as discrimination continued to exist in those practices, government-mandated quotas was a valid means of forcing employers to hire black workers, and forcing university admissions offices to accept black students. The issue further polarized the races and further fed the backlash.

Through the 1970s the backlash persisted, and it hurt all aspects of the movement. The Supreme Court, a strong supporter of civil rights at least since 1954, began to change its character during the Nixon years. In 1971 the high court ruled that cities must bus students out of their neighborhoods, if it was necessary to achieve racial integration. This decision was received with aversion in many northern cities where school districts had long been divided along racial lines. In cities like

Boston and Louisville, it was met with violence. In 1974, busing opponents won a major victory when the court, now more conservative as a result of several Nixon appointees, ruled that interdistrict busing was unconstitutional, and then offered no alternatives. The only other option was for school districts to redraw attendance zones that crossed racial lines, but the courts refused to force school districts to implement such plans, and generally none did. The result was that well over half the black students in the North, and over two-thirds in the South, continued to attend all-black schools. The *de facto* apartheid system of education continued in America, and blacks were further isolated, mostly in the inner cities, where education was poor. Then in 1978, in *Bakke v. Board of Regents of California*, the court ruled that it was unconstitutional to use quotas to achieve racial balance in the university classroom. (*See Document No. 17.*) Many of the promises held by the *Brown* decision in 1954 were negated by the mid-1970s.

The backlash hit its peak with the election of Ronald Reagan in 1980. In his campaign, Reagan succeeded in convincing a clear majority of voters that the Democrats were out of touch with traditional American values, and that their party harbored radicals, homosexuals, the undeserving poor, and the defenders of the welfare state. Race was never discussed specifically, but it was clearly the underlying theme of such Republican-raised campaign topics as inner city crime, drug abuse, illegitimacy, welfare cheats, and low educational achievement. Democrats, it seemed, had few answers to the charges.

The 1980 election was also important because it produced a group of swing voters known as Reagan Democrats, moderate Democrats (mostly white males in the eighteen-to-forty range) who deserted the Democratic party for Reagan and the Republicans. These political defectors were most likely the same disgruntled voters who supported Wallace in the late 1960s, or at least in the 1980s these voters felt the same about the nation as Wallace supporters did fifteen years before. Through the remainder of the century both political parties found it necessary to court this group. The result was that both the Democrats and the Republicans began a drift to the right, and civil rights became an issue to avoid—all to the detriment of black Americans.

In office, Reagan tried unsuccessfully to gut the Voting Rights Act. He cut funds for civil rights enforcement and the Equal Opportunity Commission, and he eliminated jobs programs, cut food stamp distribution, and health services. He also reduced welfare eligibility and removed guaranteed student loans. By the mid-1980s, the number of Americans living in poverty rose from 11 percent to nearly 14 percent. For blacks, that number jumped to over 31 percent.

Backlash as Mainstream. The Republicans rode the backlash wave through the entire decade of the 1980s, and they damaged the civil rights movement severely. The Democrats, however, barely responded. In an attempt to win back the Reagan Democrats, the Democratic party generally ignored civil rights and black issues. Through the decade, it was Jesse Jackson who carried the banner of the movement, and he carried it in the political arena, and not in the streets.

Jackson had been an important advisor to King, and then to SCLC president Ralph Abernathy after King's death in 1968. By the early 1970s, however, Jackson had broken with the SCLC to start his own organization, Operation PUSH. From there he became the most visible leader of the civil rights movement by initiating a number of economic boycotts and conducting voter registration drives. He combined the most successful aspects of the civil rights movement—politics and peaceful protest—by tying his own political campaigns for the presidency to the civil rights movement itself.

Jackson received a great deal of support from the black community in his two runs for the presidency in 1984 and 1988. But he realized that success would come only through a coalition of blacks and white liberals, and that he would have to work within the Democratic party structure. The result was the "Rainbow Coalition," Jackson's attempt to attract votes from the dispossessed of all races and groups.

Jackson's chief message was to criticize the cost of President Reagan's military buildup. He called for a 20 percent cut in the military budget, which would then free up funds to create jobs and aid the poor. In an attempt to draw organized labor into his coalition, he also opposed state right-to-work laws; and he called for a national health care plan.

In his 1984 run for the Democratic nomination, Jackson finished third behind Senators Walter Mondale and Gary Hart, both established liberals. He received 3.5 million primary votes and won several states. It was a respectable showing, and it placed him in a good position for a 1988 candidacy. But the Democratic party did not appreciate Jackson's run against the party's establishment, and even some black leaders (most notably Andrew Young and King's family members), believed that working as a pressure group within the Democratic party coalition offered a better opportunity for the future of the civil rights movement than Jackson's presidential bids.

In the 1984 general election, Reagan won easily, and with virtually no black support. White southerners, however, gave Reagan over 70 percent of their votes. The message for blacks was clear: Reagan owed them nothing. At the same time, Mondale, the Democratic candidate, ignored Jackson and civil rights issues during the campaign in an attempt to win back the Reagan Democrats, the primary personification of the backlash. Black voters responded by staying home on election day, giving Mondale a paltry 40 percent of their votes. Despite Jackson's successes, blacks did not fare well in 1984.

The situation was not much better four years later. In the 1988 primary elections, Jackson proved himself to be a mature political leader, even capable of winning elections and building a coalition including white liberals. He received twice as many votes as in 1984, finished second behind Massachusetts governor Michael Dukakis, and won primary elections across much of the South. But Jackson was snubbed by the Democrats as they again tried desperately to fight off the effects of the backlash by appealing to white middle class moderates. Jackson was passed over as Dukakis's running mate for conservative southerner, Lloyd Bentsen. In addition, Jackson was allowed little impact on the party's platform, and he was generally ignored during the campaign. The result was again predictable. Only 44 percent of blacks bothered to go to the polls. (*See Document No. 18.*)

During the 1988 general election, the Republicans unveiled a campaign strategy aimed directly at exploiting the backlash and drawing votes from the white middle class. In 1986, Willie Horton, a black convicted murderer, escaped from a weekend furlough in Massachusetts and raped a white woman in Maryland. In a widely broadcast commercial, the black, bushy-headed Horton stared into the camera as Dukakis was accused by an announcer of being soft on crime, and for supporting the Massachusetts furlough system. The message was clear: Democrats harbor black criminals.

George Bush won the election, at least in part, by being able to associate Michael Dukakis with Willie Horton. But the incident was more than just a successful political strategy. Willie Horton was a coded message for the race issue. It was designed to associate the Democratic party with civil rights, to win votes from those whites who saw the civil rights movement as having gone too far, and who saw blacks as criminals, drug abusers, and welfare cheats. Possibly more importantly, the Willie Horton commercials further connected blacks to crime in America.

Race at the Turn of the Millennium. Blacks generally did not fare well through the 1980s. By the end of the Reagan-Bush years over one-third of African Americans continued to live below the poverty line. However, as a result of changes in the tax structure during the same period, the top 1 percent of the nation saw their incomes rise by 78 percent, and the incomes for the top 5 percent increased by almost 30 percent. At the same time, the incomes for the nation's average wage earners dropped by 5 percent. For much of the country's urban black population the quality of life continued to deteriorate significantly through the decade. The black underclass was growing larger and becoming more and more isolated from the general society. There were increasing numbers of urban blacks with little education, living in poverty and despair, hooked on drugs, not seeking work, and generally unaffected by the blacks running city hall. There was clearly a growing sense of isolation and pessimism among black Americans.

By 1992 many blacks, it seemed, had lost faith in the political process to aid their plight. Black American voters made up only 8 percent of the voting population in that election, down from 10 percent in 1988. In the 1992 election, however, the winds of change had begun to shift, but not necessarily to the advantage of the nation's African Americans. President George Bush looked like a shoo-in for a second term following the Gulf War victory, but the Democratic candidate, Bill Clinton, made a major push to win back the Reagan Democrats. And that meant distancing himself as much as possible from his party's left wing, including all aspects of the civil rights movement and its leadership. Democratic party operatives had concluded that in 1988 Michael Dukakis had lost large numbers of white votes each time their candidate had appeared on the same podium with Jesse Jackson. By 1992 the Democrats had learned that lesson well—and African Americans were simply shut out. Clinton and his handlers realized that blacks would not vote Republican, and any drop in black voter strength would be easily made up by support they would pick up from whites. The strategy worked. The days of the black-vote-as-swing-vote were gone. It seemed that a predictable voting bloc with diminishing voter strength (what the white middle-class saw as representing many of the worst aspects of society) was no longer worth attention. Race was barely discussed in 1992.

Other issues and events in the nineties seemed to polarize the races even further, leaving poverty-stricken inner city blacks isolated at one end of the economic spectrum and middle-class suburban whites isolated at the other. In late April, 1992, South Central Los Angeles erupted in a major riot after four policemen were acquitted of beating black motorist, Rodney King. The attack had been video taped and shown repeatedly on television newscasts across the country. The death toll reached fifty-eight with as many as two thousand injured. The cost ranged near $1 billion. As the riots began, King went on television to appeal to the nation: "Can't we all just get along." As the riots escalated, the answer seemed to be an all-too-clear "no."

Possibly the most important aspect of the South Central riots was that nothing came of it. No leaders emerged. No movement was created. No demands were made. In fact, the riots seemed to fuel the backlash. In 1996, California voters overwhelmingly supported Proposition 209 which struck down affirmative action preferences for women and minorities in the awarding of state contracts and in determining admission to the state's universities. In 1998 Jesse Jackson accused California Governor Pete Wilson of "standing in the school house door," an obvious reference to George Wallace's stand at the University of Alabama some thirty-five years before, a stand that inaugurated the backlash.

In the 1994 midterm elections voters showed the power of the backlash by giving the Republicans a gain of fifty-one seats and control of the House of Representatives for the first time in forty years. In the Senate, Democrats lost eight seats while every Republican incumbent won easily. The chief reason for the Republican victories was a dissatisfaction with the two-year-old Clinton administration that, many apparently believed, had drifted too far to the left on a number of issues.

America's racial polarization became even more evident during the trial of O. J. Simpson. This so-called "trial of the century" that ended in October 1995 after 266 media-frenzied days, divided blacks and whites in a way they had never quite experienced before. Most black Americans believed Simpson was innocent, the victim of an unjust American legal system that had persecuted African Americans for centuries. Whites, generally, believed he was guilty, acquitted by a predominantly black jury that wanted to settle the scores of the past at the expense of the American justice system. When the verdict was read, most blacks felt they had scored a victory over an unjust system; most whites felt that the system had been subverted for the issue of race. Jesse Jackson saw how such a situation might further provoke the backlash. "It is not a time for wild celebration," he told black America. "This is a legal victory, not a moral victory for social justice. O. J. is free, but we have all been diminished during this tragedy."

Although the black radical groups of the 1960s and 1970s all died away, the Nation of Islam continued on after Malcolm's death. Under the leadership of the flamboyant Louis Farrakhan, the Nation continued to grow in numbers and influence. In the late 1980s and early 1990s, however, the Nation seemed to allow itself to be dominated by clamorous antiwhite racists and anti-Semites, overshadowing the organization's good works in the black community. By the late 1990s, the Nation of Islam seemed back on track, fighting drug abuse, crime, and poverty in the black urban community.

In October 1995, hundreds of thousands of mostly black men gathered in Washington to participate in the Million Man March. The march was inspired and organized by Farrakhan, who, as the keynote speaker, challenged black men to assume personal responsibility for themselves and their families and to become involved in the renewal of their communities. The message was a strong one. Black women, held their own march in Philadelphia in 1997. (*See Document Nos. 19 and 20.*)

Epilogue. As the century concludes, a significant part of black America has not yet reaped the benefits of the civil rights movement. For this group life remains bleak. Living primarily in the urban ghettoes, in poverty, with little or no prospect for jobs, there is a sense of isolation, pessimism, and doubt. There is no political leadership, very few educational opportunities, and for many, a weak social framework to live by. Crime in the black inner city remains high, black infant mortality rates are two-and-a-half-times that of whites, and drug abuse among African Americans continues to be a major problem. Possibly the greatest tragedy is that America, it seems, is not interested in doing much about these problems except to crack down on crime and build larger prisons to house the criminals.

Although Americans are flooded with examples of black crime, black drug abuse, and the break down in black social values, a large group of African Americans has moved quietly into the middle class, and even into affluence. It is this group that has most benefitted from the civil rights movement.

In the opposite corner is the backlash. With its antecedents in the mid-1960s, it is a large movement that began by pushing against the excesses of sixties liberalism and continues on in opposition to social, political, and economic liberalism. It is religious, moral, conservative, and powerful. It is also broad, and strong enough to be an influential factor in both political parties. Race was always at the core of the backlash, and clearly race continues, in many ways, to be the bond that keeps the backlash together. The leaders of the backlash have exploited the anger of white middle-class taxpayers who believe their taxes are going to the undeserved poor, particularly young black women, without education, who are long-term dependents and whose dependency is passed on from one generation to another.

The backlash has been debilitating to the civil rights movement. At times it has worked to halt civil rights advances; at other times it has stifled civil rights reforms. It has forced both political parties to turn away from civil rights, away from black leaders, away from black issues, and to answer the call of those who believe, at their worst, that blacks do not deserve an equal place in society; and, at their best, that the status quo is adequate. As long as the backlash flourishes, African Americans in the general society can expect setbacks, while the nation's inner cities will continue their plight.

The First Reconstruction failed because blacks could not control their own economic fate; they remained dependent on the white economic structure in the South. Without that control they could not manage their political lives or control their place in the social system. The result was disenfranchisement and finally segregation. The Second Reconstruction saw limited success. The civil rights movement forced the federal government to impose laws (primarily the Civil Rights Act of 1964 and the Voting Rights Act of 1965) that brought an end to legalized segregation and disenfranchisement in the South. That movement had its successes because of strong leadership, a determined black population, the sympathy of a politically dominant northern white liberal political constituency, and a sympathetic (if often self-serving) White House.

But determination, government support, and liberal money could not push the civil rights movement much beyond the successes of the mid-1960s. The result was an understandable frustration and pessimism that in turn allowed for a leadership to emerge that took the movement in the directions of radicalism, black nationalism, and ultimately violence in the streets. The inevitable reaction was a debilitating backlash. Weak at first, even to the point of aiding the cause of civil rights, the backlash gained enormous momentum as the nation swung into a conservative mode in the two decades after King's death. Liberal money dried up, the civil rights leadership fragmented, and candidates in both parties found it politically expedient to desert civil rights and black causes in favor of a more conservative constituency. As the century closed, the black image in the American mind was not a good one, and the backlash raged on. But many black Americans, possibly approaching half the black population, have moved into middle-class America. As their conditions continue to improve, and as they continue an agonizingly slow pace toward equality, they remain the hope for the future of black America.

PART II

DOCUMENTS

DOCUMENT NO. 1

GUNNAR MYRDAL AND THE "NEGRO PROBLEM"*

In 1944 Swedish sociologist Gunnar Myrdal published An American Dilemma, *a study of what was called at the time, "the Negro problem." The dilemma that Myrdal perceived was the moral conflict in the American mind between race discrimination and the American creed of equality for all. The "problem," as Myrdal explained it, was a moral problem for whites, caused by whites, and finally perpetuated by whites.*

γ　　　　　γ　　　　　γ

There is a "Negro problem" in the United States and most Americans are aware of it, although it assumes varying forms and intensity in different regions of the country and among diverse groups of the American people. Americans have to react to it, politically as citizens and, where there are Negroes present in the community, privately as neighbors.

To the great majority of white Americans the Negro problem has distinctly negative connotations. It suggests something difficult to settle and equally difficult to leave alone. It is embarrassing. It makes for moral uneasiness. The very presence of the Negro in America, his fate in this country through slavery, Civil War and Reconstruction, his recent career and his present status, his accommodation, his protest and his aspiration, in fact his entire biological, historical and social existence as a participant American represent to the ordinary white man in the North as well as in the South an anomaly in the very structure of American society. To many, this takes on the proportion of a menace— biological, economic, social, cultural, and, at times political. This anxiety may be mingled with a feeling of individual and collective guilt. A few see the problem as a challenge to statesmanship. To all it is a trouble.

These and many other mutually inconsistent attitudes are blended into none too logical a scheme which, in turn, may be quite inconsistent with the wider personal, moral, religious, and civic sentiments and ideas of the Americans. Now and then, even the least sophisticated individual

*Source: Gunnar Myrdal, *An American Dilemma: The Negro Problem and Modern Democracy* (New York: Harper and Row, 1944), pp. lxix–lxxv.

becomes aware of his own confusion and the contradiction in his attitudes. . . . But most people, most of the time, suppress such threats to
their moral integrity together with all of the confusion, the ambiguity,
and inconsistency which lurks in the basement of man's soul. This,
however, is rarely accomplished without mental strain. . . .

The strain is increased in democratic America by the freedom left
open—even in the South, to a considerable extent—for the advocates
of the Negro, his rights and welfare. All "pro-Negro" forces in American society, whether organized or not, and irrespective of their wide differences in both strategy and tactics, sense that this is the situation.
They all work on the national conscience. They all seek to fix everybody's attention on the suppressed moral conflict. No wonder that they
are often regarded as public nuisances. . . .

The American Negro problem is a problem in the heart of the American. It is there that the interracial tension has its focus. It is there that
the decisive struggle goes on. This is the central view point of this trea-
tise. Though our study includes economic, social, and political race
relations, at bottom our problem is the moral dilemma of the American—the conflict between his moral valuations on various levels of consciousness and generality. The "American Dilemma," referred to in the
title of this book, is the ever-raging conflict between, on the one hand,
the valuations preserved on the general plane which we shall call the
"American Creed," where the American thinks, talks, and acts under
the influence of high national and Christian precepts, and, on the other
hand, the valuations on specific planes of individual and group living,
where personal and local interests; economic, social and sexual jealous-
ies; considerations of community prestige and conformity; group prejudice against particular persons or types of people; and all sorts of mis-
cellaneous wants, impulses, and habits dominate his outlook. . . .

The Negro problem in America would be of a different nature, and,
indeed, would be simpler to handle scientifically, if the moral conflict
raged only between valuations held by different persons and groups of
persons. The essence of the moral situation is, however, that the con-
flicting valuations are also held by the same person. The moral struggle
goes on within people and not only between them. . . . The unity of a
culture consists in the fact that all valuations are mutually shared in
sonic degree. We shall find that even a poor and uneducated white person in some isolated and backward rural region in the Deep South, who
is violently prejudiced against the Negro and intent upon depriving him

of civic rights and human independence, has also a whole compartment in his valuation sphere housing the entire American creed of liberty, equality, justice, and fair opportunity for everybody. He is actually also a good Christian and honestly devoted to the ideals of human brotherhood and the Golden Rule. And these more general valuations—more general in the sense that they refer to all human beings—are, to some extent, effective in shaping his behavior. Indeed, it would be impossible to understand why the Negro does not fare worse in some regions of America if it were not constantly kept in mind that behavior is the outcome of a compromise between valuations, among which the equalitarian ideal is one. At the other end, there are few liberals, even in New England, who have not a well-furnished compartment of race prejudice, even if it is usually suppressed from conscious attention. Even the American Negroes share in this community of valuations: they have eagerly imbibed the American Creed and the revolutionary Christian teaching of common brotherhood; under closer study, they usually reveal also that they hold something of the majority prejudice against their own characteristics. . . .

Although the Negro problem is a moral issue both to Negroes and to whites, we shall in this book have to give primary attention to what goes on in the minds of white Americans. To explain this direction of our interest a general conclusion from our study needs to be stated at this point. When the present investigator started his inquiry, his preconception was that it had to be focused on the Negro people and their peculiarities. This is understandable since, from a superficial view, Negro Americans, not only in physical appearance, but also in thoughts, feelings, and in manner of life, seemed stranger to him than did white Americans. Furthermore, most of the literature on the Negro problem dealt with the Negroes: their racial and cultural characteristics, their living standards. . . . But as he proceeded in his studies into the Negro problem, it became increasingly evident that little, if anything, could be scientifically explained in terms of the peculiarities of the Negroes themselves. As a matter of fact, in their basic human traits the Negroes are inherently not much different from other people. Neither are, incidently, the white Americans. But Negroes and whites in the United States live in singular human relations with each other. All the circumstances of life—the "environmental" conditions in the broadest meaning of that term—diverge more from the "normal" for the Negroes than for the whites, if only because of the statistical fact that the Negroes are the smaller group. The average Negro must experience many times more of the "abnormal" interracial relations than the average white man in America. The more important fact, however, is that practically all the economic, social, and political power is held by whites. The Negroes do not by far have anything approaching a tenth of the things worth having in America.

It is thus the white majority group that naturally determines the Negro's "place." All our attempts to reach scientific explanations of why the Negroes are what they are and why they live as they do have regularly led to determinants on the white side of the race line. In the practical and political struggles of effecting changes, the views and attitudes of the white Americans are likewise strategic. The Negro's entire life, and consequently, also his opinions on the Negro problem, are, in the main, to be considered as secondary reactions to more primary pressures from the side of the dominant white majority.

DOCUMENT NO. 2

THEODORE BILBO AND THE
PHILOSOPHY OF SOUTHERN RACISM
MARCH 22, 1944*

Mississippi politician Theodore Bilbo was a rabid racist, possibly the most openly racist public figure of his time. Known as "The Man," Bilbo considered it his responsibility to keep Mississippi segregated at all costs—at least in part to stop, what he often called, the mongrelization of the white race. Bilbo served as Mississippi governor from 1916 to 1920 and than again from 1928 to 1932. He was elected to the U.S. Senate in 1935 and served there until his death in 1947. In the selection below Bilbo speaks to a joint session of the Mississippi legislature in opposition to a move in the U.S. Senate to abolish the poll tax.

γ   γ   γ

The so-called leaders of the Negro race have deliberately chosen this time of war to launch their program of full equality of the races in this country. The March-on-Washington movement, a Negro group headed by A. Philip Randolph, president of the Brotherhood of Sleeping Car Porters, carried their demands to the White House in June 1941. Thousands of Negroes threatened to march in mass upon Washington in what they termed "protest of discrimination in Government employment and in the war industries." After conferences with the Negro leaders, President Roosevelt issued Executive Order 8802 and the march on Washington was called off. This order, issued June 25, 1941, provided that:

> There shall be no discrimination in the employment of workers in defense industries or Government because of race, creed, color, or national origin.

The order also established the Committee on Fair Employment Practices to carry this policy into effect. There is nothing in Executive Order 8802 about abolishing segregation and ordering the mixing of the races. However, as a result of the order there is today no segregation in the United States Government offices in Washington.

*Source: Congressional Record, Vol. XC, pt. 9, 78th Cong. 2d sess. (Washington, D.C., USGPO, 1944), pp. A1795–A1802.

In the Federal offices in Washington, whites and Negroes work in the same rooms, the same offices, eat together at the same cafeterias, use the same rest rooms and recreational facilities. White girls may be assigned as secretaries to Negro men, and Negro girls may be sent to the offices of white officials. . . . In many bureaus and departments, the mixing of the races has gone so far that southern girls going to the capital city to work, have returned to their homes. Others, who for various reasons must remain there to work, find such conditions almost unbearable. . . .

I am sure you have read in the Jackson [Mississippi] Daily News of Wednesday, March 8, the Washington story of Dr. Studebaker and his Negro assistant, Dr. Ambrose Caliver, calling on the colleges and universities of the South to open wide their doors for the matriculation of Negro students. . . . [The Daily News] editorial on this report from the Office of Education out of Washington, under the title of "Go Straight to Hell," meets with my full and complete endorsement. [The editor] is right when he says that the South won't do it and that not in this generation and never in the future while Anglo-Saxon blood flows in our veins will the people of the South open the doors of their colleges and universities for Negro students. I repeat that [the editor] is right. We will tell our Negro-loving Yankee friends to go straight to hell.

Another group of Negroes recently sounded the warning that they would use force if necessary to will the full equality that they are seeking. This group visited me in my office in Washington shortly after I became chairman of the Senate Committee on the District of Columbia. Practically every Negro organization in Washington had a representative in the group, and they wanted me to know the demands which they were making for full political, economic, and social equality. When I expressed my doubts as to their receiving what they were asking, one spokesman said that if that were true, then Negroes had just as well quit buying War bonds and get out of the war effort. It was further said by one member of the group that Negroes intended to secure full equality and would do so by force, if necessary, when the war is over. There you have their demands in no uncertain terms. . . .

In February the C.I.O. opened a canteen in Washington for service men and women. . . . On opening night there were some 200 service men and women present. There were about an equal number of white and Negro soldiers who attended and white girls and Negro girls served as hostesses to those soldiers in equal numbers. Can you picture such social affairs taking place in our Nation's Capital? . . . . Have we reached the place in this country when we are going to permit our white girls to attend social functions with Negro soldiers? If we do permit such, can we profess to be surprised at what the results may be? . . . Are our soldiers and sailors fighting to save this Nation, or are they fighting so that we may become a mongrelized people? Practicing social equality of the races is certainly the surest way to destroy the culture of the white race. . . .

We in the Southland, being fully aware of the attempts to break down segregation and implant social equality of the races throughout the Nation are ready to do some plain talking. The Negro leaders have brought this issue of race relations before us in this time of war; they have stated their demands so we have no alternative but to tell them where we stand.

We in Mississippi are justly proud of the harmonious relations existing here among the races. Our population is almost equally divided and we are glad to have peaceful, law-abiding Negroes within our midst. We ask no Negro to leave our State; at the same time we ask no discontented Negro to remain.

Three-fourths of the Nation's 12,800,000 Negroes are living and earning a livelihood in the South. We have an established policy of segregation known and understood by the members of both races. We recognize the right of a Negro to hire Negroes in preference to white people and the white employer has the same right. The right of Southern white people to operate political associations and hold their primaries, excluding Negroes, is no more to be questioned than the right of Negroes to form political or social clubs, excluding white people. Certainly Negroes may own and conduct their own restaurants, hotels and shops exclusively for themselves, just as white people may do likewise. The races shall have equal and separate accommodations on busses and trains; and separate public schools shall be maintained. Equal and exact justice shall be accorded both races under the law, but segregation of the races shall be enforced. Honest and intelligent Southern white and colored people agree with this policy. . . .

The superior ability of the Caucasian man is evidenced by his endless creation of art, science, law, religion, literature, and every other form of activity known to man down through the ages. Against these achievements, what has the African to offer? What history? What art? What science? What morality? And who will deny the almightiness of heredity? Let the blood stream be corrupted and nothing can ever restore its purity. If you do not accept this as true, then you brand as false both history and biology. . . .

History clearly shows that the white race is the custodian of the gospel of Jesus Christ and that the white man is entrusted with the spreading of that gospel.

The gospel, of course, is universal; it is missionary in scope; and it is given to all men of all nations. Yet what can be more foreign to the ideals of the Christian religion than amalgamation and miscegenation? Anyone who would, in the name of Christianity, make us a negroid people betrays his religion and his race.

It should be the desire of both races to maintain racial integrity and have their blood remain pure. If religion teaches the destruction of the races and commits the error of preaching the mixture of all bloods, then what can the missionaries and ministers do to give to the unborn generations the racial heritage which is rightfully theirs?. . . .

There are those who would tear away [the] racial pride [of Southern whites], knowing full well that it would plunge the Southland into hopeless depths of hybridization. Implant the doctrines of social equality below the Mason-Dixon line, and the result will be a mongrelized Southland. And if the transmitted germ plasma is destroyed, nothing shall ever restore it; neither wealth, nor culture, nor science, nor art, nor morality, nor religion itself.

To southerners this is not a question of individual morality or of self-respect or of individual accomplishments. Every child that is born is born not only of its immediate parents but of all its ancestry. Every child is a child of its race, and heredity plays its part upon it and upon all its descendants. However weak the white man, behind him stands Europe; however strong the black, behind him lies Africa. . . .

We people of the South must draw the color line tighter and tighter, and any white man or woman who dares to cross that color line should be promptly and forever ostracized. No compromise on this great question should be tolerated, no matter who the guilty parties are, whether in the church, in public office, or in the private walks of life. Ostracize them if they cross the color line and treat them as a Negro or as his equal should be treated. . . .

It is imperative that we face squarely and frankly the conditions which confront us. We must not sit idly by, but we must ever be on guard to protect the southern ideals, customs, and traditions that we love and believe in so firmly and completely. There are some issues that we may differ upon, but on racial integrity, white supremacy, and love of the Southland we will stand together until we pass on to another world.

DOCUMENT NO. 3

*TO SECURE THESE RIGHTS**

President Truman created the President's Committee on Civil Rights in December 1946. The committee was created at least partly in response to a series of violent acts against blacks in the South. Many of the victims were veterans. The committee was instructed to recommend ways in which the several levels of government might be strengthened to bring an end to racial discrimination. The result was the committee's report, To Secure These Rights. *Many of the committee's recommendations were incorporated in the Truman's civil rights message to Congress in February 1948.*

γ   γ   γ

The Condition of Our Rights

The Crime of Lynching In 1946 at least six persons in the United States were lynched by mobs. Three of them had not been charged, either by the police or anyone else, with an offense. . . .

While available statistics show that, decade by decade, lynchings have decreased, this Committee has found that in the year 1947 lynching remains one of the most serious threats to the civil rights of Americans. It is still possible for a mob to abduct and murder a person in some sections of the country with almost certain assurance of escaping punishment for the crime. The decade from 1936 through 1946 saw at least 43 lynchings. No person received the death penalty, and the majority of the guilty persons were not even prosecuted.

The communities in which lynchings occur tend to condone the crime. Punishment of lynchers is not accepted as the responsibility of state or local governments in these communities. Frequently, state officials participate in the crime, actively or passively. Federal efforts to punish the crime are resisted. Condonation of lynching is indicated by the failure of some local law enforcement officials to make adequate efforts to break up a mob. It is further shown by failure in most cases to make any real effort to apprehend or try those guilty. If the federal gov-

Source: To Secure These Rights: The Report of the President's Committee on Civil Rights (New York, 1947), ix, x–xi, 20, 22, 23–24, 25, 27, 35, 55–56, 57, 99, 102–103.

ernment enters a case, local officials sometimes actively resist the federal investigation. . . .

POLICE BRUTALITY

We have reported the failure of some public officials to fulfill their most elementary duty—the protection of persons against mob violence. We must also report more widespread and varied forms of official misconduct. These include violent physical attacks by police officers on members of minority groups, the use of third degree methods to extort confessions, and brutality against prisoners. Civil rights violations of this kind are by no means universal and many law enforcement agencies have gone far in recent years toward stamping out these evils. . . .

The total picture—adding the connivance of some police officials in lynchings to their record of brutality against Negroes in other situations—is, in the opinion of this Committee, a serious reflection on American justice. We know that Americans everywhere deplore this violence. We recognize further that there are many law enforcement officers in the South and the North who do not commit violent acts against Negroes or other friendless culprits. We are convinced, however, that the incidence of police brutality against Negroes is disturbingly high. . . .

THE RIGHT TO VOTE

The right of all qualified citizens to vote is today considered axiomatic by most Americans. To achieve universal adult suffrage we have carried on vigorous political crusades since the earliest days of the Republic. In theory the aim has been achieved, but in fact there are many backwaters in our political life were the right to vote is not assured to every qualified citizen. The franchise is barred to some citizens because of race; to others by institutions or procedures which impede free access to the polls. Still other Americans are in substance disfranchised whenever electoral irregularities or corrupt practices dissipate their votes or distort their intended purpose. . . .

The denial of the suffrage on account of race is the most serious present interference with the right to vote. Until very recently, American Negro citizens in most southern states found it difficult to vote. Some Negroes have voted in parts of the upper South for the last twenty years. In recent years the situation in the deep South has changed to the point where it can be said that Negroes are beginning to exercise the political rights of free Americans. In the light of history, this represents progress, limited and precarious, but nevertheless progress. . . .

Discriminatory hiring practices.—Discrimination is most acutely felt by minority group members in their inability to get a job suited to their qualifications. Exclusions of Negroes, Jews, or Mexicans in the process of hiring is effected in various ways—by newspaper advertisements requesting only whites or gentiles to apply, by registration or application blanks on which a space is reserved for "race" or "religion," by discriminatory job orders placed with employment agencies, or by the arbitrary policy of a company official in charge of hiring. . . .

On-the-job discrimination.—If he can get himself hired, the minority worker often finds that he is being paid less than other workers. This wage discrimination is sharply evident in studies made of individual cities and is especially exaggerated in the South. A survey, conducted by the Research and Information Department of the American Federation of Labor shows that the average weekly income of white veterans ranges from 30 to 78 percent above the average income of Negro veterans in 26 communities, 25 of them in the South. In Houston, for example, 36,000 white veterans had a weekly income of $49 and 4,000 Negro veterans had average incomes of $30—a difference of 63 percent. These differences are not caused solely by the relegation of the Negroes to lower types of work, but reflect wage discriminations between whites and Negroes for the same type of work. The Final Report of the FEPC states that the hourly wage rates for Negro common laborers averaged 47.4 cents in July, 1942, as compared with 65.3 cents for white laborers. . . .

Government's Responsibility: Securing the Rights

The National Government of the United States must take the lead in safeguarding the civil rights of all Americans. We believe that this is one of the most important observations that can be made about the civil rights problem in our country today. . . .

Leadership by the federal government in safeguarding civil rights does not mean exclusive action by that government. There is much that the states and local communities can do in this field, and much that they alone can do. The Committee believes that Justice Holmes' view of the states as 48 laboratories for social and economic experimentation is still valid. The very complexity of the civil rights problem calls for much experimental, remedial action which may be better undertaken by the states than by the national government. Parallel state and local action supporting the national program is highly desirable. It is obvious that even though the federal government should take steps to stamp out the crime of lynching, the states cannot escape the responsibility to employ all of the powers and resources available to them for the same end. Or again, the enactment of a federal fair employment practice act will not render similar state legislation unnecessary.

In certain areas the states must do far more than parallel federal action. Either for constitutional or administrative reasons, they must remain the primary protectors of civil rights. This is true of governmental efforts to control or outlaw racial or religious discrimination practiced by privately supported public-service institutions such as schools and hospitals, and of places of public accommodation such as hotels, restaurants, theaters, and stores.

Furthermore, government action alone, whether federal, state, local, or all combined, cannot provide complete protection of civil rights. Everything that government does stems from and is conditioned by the state of public opinion. Civil rights in this country will never be adequately protected until the intelligent will of the American people approves and demands that protection. Great responsibility, therefore, will always rest upon private organizations and private individuals who are in a position to educate and shape public opinion. The argument is sometimes made that because prejudice and intolerance cannot be eliminated through legislation and government control we should abandon that action in favor of the long, slow, evolutionary effects of education and voluntary private efforts. We believe that this argument misses the point and that the choice it poses between legislation and education as to the means of improving civil rights is an unnecessary one. In our opinion, both approaches to the goal are valid, and are, moreover, essential to each other.

DOCUMENT NO. 4

BROWN V. BOARD OF EDUCATION
MAY 17, 1954*

In 1953 Earl Warren was named Chief Justice of the United States Supreme Court by President Dwight Eisenhower. On May 17, 1954, the now Chief Justice wrote the following landmark decision of Oliver Brown v. Board of Education of Topeka Kansas.

γ   γ   γ

These cases come to us from the States of Kansas, South Carolina, Virginia, and Delaware. They are premised on different facts and different local conditions, but a common legal question justifies their consideration together in this consolidated opinion.

In each of the cases, minors of the Negro race, through their legal representatives, seek the aid of the courts in obtaining admission to the public schools of their community on a nonsegregated basis. In each instance, they had been denied admission to schools attended by white children under laws requiring or permitting segregation according to race. This segregation was alleged to deprive the plaintiffs of the equal protection of the laws under the Fourteenth Amendment. In each of the cases other than the Delaware case, a three-judge federal district court denied relief to the plaintiffs on the so-called "separate but equal" doctrine announced by this Court in *Plessy* v. *Ferguson*, 163 U.S. 537. Under that doctrine, equality of treatment is accorded when the races are provided substantially equal facilities, even though these facilities be separate. . . .

The plaintiffs contend that segregated public schools are not "equal" and cannot be made "equal," and that hence they are deprived of the equal protection of the laws. Because of the obvious importance of the question presented, the Court took jurisdiction. Argument was heard in the 1952 Term, and reargument was heard this Term on certain questions propounded by the Court.

Reargument was largely devoted to the circumstances surrounding the adoption of the Fourteenth Amendment in 1868. It covered exhaustively consideration of the Amendment in Congress, ratification by the

*Source: 347 U.S., 483, 1954.

states, then existing practices in racial segregation, and the views of proponents and opponents of the Amendment. This discussion and our own investigation convince us that, although these sources cast some light, it is not enough to resolve the problem with which we are faced. At best, they are inconclusive. The most avid proponents of the post-War Amendments undoubtedly intended them to remove all legal distinctions among "all persons born or naturalized in the United States." Their opponents, just as certainly, were antagonistic to both the letter and the spirit of the Amendments and wished them to have the most limited effect. What others in Congress and the state legislature had in mind cannot be determined with any degree of certainty.

An additional reason for the inconclusive nature of the Amendment's history, with respect to segregated schools, is the status of public education at that time. In the South, the movement toward free common schools, supported by general taxation, had not yet taken hold. Education of white children was largely in the hands of private groups. Education of Negroes was almost non-existent, and practically all of the race were illiterate. In fact, any education of Negroes was forbidden by law in some states. Today, in contrast, many Negroes have achieved outstanding success in the arts and sciences as well as in the business and professional world. It is true that public school education at the time of the Amendment had advanced further in the North, but the effect of the Amendment on Northern States was generally ignored in the congressional debates. Even in the North, the conditions of public education did not approximate those existing today. The curriculum was usually rudimentary; ungraded schools were common in rural areas; the school term was but three months a year in many states; and compulsory school attendance was virtually unknown. As a consequence, it is not surprising that there should be so little in the history of the Fourteenth Amendment relating to its intended effect on public education.

In the first cases in this Court construing the Fourteenth Amendment, decided shortly after its adoption, the Court interpreted it as proscribing all state-imposed discriminations against the Negro race. The doctrine of "separate but equal" did not make its appearance in this Court until 1896 in the case of *Plessy* v. *Ferguson, supra,* involving not education but transportation. American courts have since labored with the doctrine for over half a century. In this Court, there have been six cases involving the "separate but equal" doctrine in the field of public education. In *Cumming* v. *County Board of Education*, 175 U.S. 528, and

Gong Lum v. *Rice*, 275 U.S. 78, the validity of the doctrine itself was not challenged. In more recent cases, all on the graduate school level, inequality was found in that specific benefits enjoyed by white students were denied to Negro students of the same educational qualifications. . . .

In approaching this problem, we cannot turn the clock back to 1868 when the Amendment was adopted, or even to 1896 when *Plessy* v. *Ferguson* was written. We must consider public education in the light of its full development and its present place in American life throughout the Nation. Only in this way can it be determined if segregation in public schools deprives these plaintiffs of the equal protection of the laws.

Today, education is perhaps the most important function of state and local governments. Compulsory school attendance laws and the great expenditures for education both demonstrate our recognition of the importance of education to our democratic society. It is required in the performance of our most basic public responsibilities, even service in the armed forces. It is the very foundation of good citizenship. Today it is a principal instrument in awakening the child to cultural values, in preparing him for later professional training, and in helping him to adjust normally to his environment. In these days, it is doubtful that any child may reasonably be expected to succeed in life if he is denied the opportunity of an education. Such an opportunity, where the state has undertaken to provide it, is a right which must be made available to all on equal terms.

We come then to the question presented: Does segregation of children in public schools solely on the basis of race, even though the physical facilities and other "tangible" factors may be equal, deprive the children of the minority group of equal educational opportunities? We believe that it does.

In *Sweatt* v. *Painter*, *supra*, in finding that a segregated law school for Negroes could not provide them equal educational opportunities, this Court relied in large part on "those qualities which are incapable of objective measurement but which make for greatness in a law school." In *McLaurin* v. *Oklahoma State Regents*, *supra*, the Court, in requiring that a Negro admitted to a white graduate school be treated like all other students, again resorted to intangible considerations: ". . . . his ability to study, to engage in discussions and exchange views with other students, and, in general, to learn his profession." Such considerations apply with added force to children in grade and high schools. To separate them from others of similar age and qualifications solely because of their race generates a feeling of inferiority as to their status in the community that may affect their hearts and minds in a way unlikely ever to be undone. The effect of this separation on their educational opportunities was well stated by a finding in the Kansas case by a court which nevertheless felt compelled to rule against the Negro plaintiffs:

"Segregation of white and colored children in public schools has a detrimental effect upon the colored children. The impact is greater when it has the sanction of the law; for the policy of separating the races is usually interpreted as denoting the inferiority of the negro group. A sense of inferiority affects the motivation of a child to learn. Segregation with the sanction of law, therefore, has a tendency to [retard] the educational and mental development of negro children and to deprive them of some of the benefits they would receive in a racial[ly] integrated school system."

Whatever may have been the extent of psychological knowledge at the time of *Plessy* v. *Ferguson*, this finding is amply supported by modern authority. Any language in *Plessy* v. *Ferguson* contrary to this finding is rejected.

We conclude that in the field of public education the doctrine of "separate but equal" has no place. Separate educational facilities are inherently unequal. Therefore, we hold that the plaintiffs and others similarly situated for whom the actions have been brought are, by reason of the segregation complained of, deprived of the equal protection of the laws guaranteed by the Fourteenth Amendment. This disposition makes unnecessary any discussion whether such segregation also violates the Due Process Clause of the Fourteenth Amendment.

Because these are class actions, because of the wide applicability of this decision, and because of the great variety of local conditions, the formulation of decrees in these cases presents problems of considerable complexity. On reargument, the consideration of appropriate relief was necessarily subordinated to the primary question—the constitutionality of segregation in public education. We have now announced that such segregation is a denial of the equal protection of the laws. . . .

DOCUMENT NO. 5

ROSA PARKS'S STORY*

On December 1, 1955, Rosa Parks was told to relinquish her seat on a Montgomery city bus to a white patron—as required by city ordinance. She refused. The result was the Montgomery bus boycott, one of the most important events in the history of the civil rights movement. Below is her account of the events.

γ   γ   γ

I knew [the NAACP] needed a plaintiff who was beyond reproach, because I was in on the discussions about the possible court cases. But that is not why I refused to give up my bus seat to a white man on Thursday, December 1, 1955. I did not intend to get arrested. If I had been paying attention, I wouldn't even have gotten on that bus.

I was very busy at that particular time. I was getting an NAACP workshop together for the 3rd or 4th of December, and I was trying to get the consent of Mr. H. Council Trenholm at Alabama State to have the Saturday meeting at the college. He did give permission, but I had a hard time getting to him to get permission to use the building. I was also getting notices in the mail for the election of officers of the Senior Branch of the NAACP, which would be the next week.

When I got off from work that evening of December 1, I went to Court Square as usual to catch the Cleveland Avenue bus home. I didn't look to see who was driving when I got on, and by the time I recognized him, I had already paid my fare. It was the same driver who had put me off the bus back in 1943, twelve years earlier. He was still tall and heavy, with red, rough-looking skin. And he was still mean-looking. I didn't know if he had been on that route before—they switched the drivers around sometimes. I do know that most of the time if I saw him on a bus, I wouldn't get on it.

I saw a vacant seat in the middle section of the bus and took it. I didn't even question why there was a vacant seat even though there were quite a few people standing in the back. If I had thought about it at all, I would probably have figured maybe someone saw me get on and did

*Source: Rosa Parks with Jim Haskins, *Rosa Parks: My Story* (New York: Dial Books, 1992).

not take the seat but left it vacant for me. There was a man sitting next to the window and two women across the aisle.

The next stop was the Empire Theater, and some whites got on. They filled up the white seats, and one man was left standing. The driver looked back and noticed the man standing. Then he looked back at us. He said, "Let me have those front seats," because they were the front seats of the black section. Didn't anybody move. We just sat right where we were, the four of us. Then he spoke a second time: "Y'all better make it light on yourselves and let me have those seats."

The man in the window seat next to me stood up, and I moved to let him pass me, and then I looked across the aisle and saw the two women were also standing. I moved over to the window seat. I could not see how standing up was going to "make it light" for me. The more we gave in and complied, the worse they treated us. . . .

The driver of the bus saw me still sitting there, and he asked was I going to stand up. I said, "No." He said, "Well, I'm going to have you arrested." Then I said, "You may do that." These were the only words we said to each other. . . .

As I sat there, I tried not to think about what might happen. I knew anything was possible. I could be manhandled or beaten. I could be arrested. People have asked me if it occurred to me then that I could be the test case the NAACP had been looking for. I did not think that at all. In fact if I had let myself think too deeply about what might happen to me, I might have gotten off the bus. But I chose to remain.

DOCUMENT NO. 6

SOUTHERN LEGISLATORS REPLY TO THE *BROWN* DECISION*

In March 1956 over one hundred southern congressmen and senators signed the Declaration of Constitutional Principles, better known as the Southern Manifesto. The document evoked many of the old southern responses to federal authority, while mostly ignoring the race issue. In 1956 it represented the objections of many white southerners to the Brown *decision.*

ɣ   ɣ   ɣ

The unwarranted decision of the Supreme Court in the public school cases is now bearing the fruit always produced when men substitute naked power for established law.

The Founding Fathers gave us a Constitution of checks and balances because they realized the inescapable lesson of history that no man or group of men can be safely entrusted with unlimited power. They framed this Constitution with its provisions for change by amendment in order to secure the fundamentals of government against the dangers of temporary popular passion or the personal predilections of public officeholders.

We regard the decision of the Supreme Court in the school cases as a clear abuse of judicial power. It climaxes a trend in the Federal Judiciary undertaking to legislate, in derogation of the authority of Congress, and to encroach upon the reserved rights of the States and the people.

The original Constitution does not mention education. Neither does the 14th amendment nor any other amendment. The debates preceding the submission of the 14th amendment clearly show that there was no intent that it should affect the system of education maintained by the States. . . .

In the case of *Plessy* v. *Ferguson* in 1896 the Supreme Court expressly declared that under the 14th amendment no person was denied any of his rights if the States provided separate but equal public facilities. This decision has been followed in many other cases. It is notable that the Supreme Court, speaking through Chief Justice Taft, a former Presi-

*Source: *Congressional Record*, 84th Cong., 2d sess., March 12, 1956, pp. 4460–4461.

dent of the United States, unanimously declared in 1927 in *Lum v. Rice* that the "separate but equal" principle is "within the discretion of the State in regulating its public schools and does not conflict with the 14th amendment."

This interpretation, restated time and again, became a part of the life of the people of many of the States and confirmed their habits, customs, traditions, and way of life. It is founded on elemental humanity and commonsense, for parents should not be deprived by Government of the right to direct the lives and education of their own children.

Though there has been no constitutional amendment or act of Congress changing this established legal principle almost a century old, the Supreme Court of the United States, with no legal basis for such action, undertook to exercise their naked judicial power and substituted their personal political and social ideas for the established law of the land.

This unwarranted exercise of power by the Court, contrary to the Constitution, is creating chaos and confusion in the States principally affected. It is destroying the amicable relations between the white and Negro races that have been created through 90 years of patient effort by the good people of both races. It has planted hatred and suspicion where there has been heretofore friendship and understanding.

Without regard to the consent of the governed, outside agitators are threatening immediate and revolutionary changes in our public-school systems. If done, this is certain to destroy the system of public education in some of the States.

With the gravest concern for the explosive and dangerous condition created by this decision and inflamed by outside meddlers:

We reaffirm our reliance on the Constitution as the fundamental law of the land.

We decry the Supreme Court's encroachments on rights reserved to the States and to the people, contrary to established law, and to the Constitution.

We commend the motives of those States which have declared the intention to resist forced integration by any lawful means.

We appeal to the States and people who are not directly affected by these decisions to consider the constitutional principles involved against the time when they too, on issues vital to them, may be the victims of judicial encroachment.

Even though we constitute a minority in the present Congress, we have full faith that a majority of the American people believe in the dual system of government which has enabled us to achieve our greatness and will in time demand that the reserved rights of the States and of the people be made secure against judicial usurpation.

We pledge ourselves to use all lawful means to bring about a reversal of this decision which is contrary to the Constitution and to prevent the use of force in its implementation.

In this trying period, as we all seek to right this wrong, we appeal to our people not to be provoked by the agitators and troublemakers invading our States and to scrupulously refrain from disorder and lawless acts.

DOCUMENT NO. 7

LETTER FROM A BIRMINGHAM JAIL*

Martin Luther King, Jr., conducted a series of marches in Birmingham in the spring of 1963 with the intention of forcing that city to desegregate its government offices and public facilities. On April 12 he was arrested and jailed for defying a court order. In response to King's actions, eight white clergymen in Birmingham denounced King as an extremist and advised blacks to withdraw their support for his movement. King attacked the clergymen in his "Letter from a Birmingham Jail." He also criticized the nation's white moderates for denying their support to the civil rights movement. He also warned that black nationalism might take over the movement if he failed.

γ   γ   γ

You may well ask: "Why direct action? Why sit-ins, marches and so forth? Isn't negotiation a better path?" You are quite right in calling for negotiation. Indeed, this is the very purpose of direct action. Nonviolent direct action seeks to create such a crisis and foster such a tension that a community which has constantly refused to negotiate is forced to confront the issue. It seeks so to dramatize the issue that it can no longer be ignored. My citing the creation of tension as part of the work of the nonviolent-resister may sound rather shocking. But I must confess that I am not afraid of the word "tension." I have earnestly opposed violent tension, but there is a type of constructive, nonviolent tension which is necessary for growth. Just as Socrates felt that it was necessary to create a tension in the mind so that individuals could rise from the bondage of myths and half-truths to the unfettered realm of creative analysis and objective appraisal, so must we see the need for nonviolent gadflies to create the kind of tension in society that will help men rise from the

*Source: Martin Luther King, Jr., *Why We Can't Wait* (New York: 1964), pp. 77–100. Reprinted by arrangement with The Heirs to the Estate of Martin Luther King, Jr., c/o Writers House, Inc. as agent for the proprietor.

dark depths of prejudice and racism to the majestic heights of understanding and brotherhood.

The purpose of our direct-action program is to create a situation so crisis-packed that it will inevitably open the door to negotiation. I therefore concur with you in your call for negotiation. Too long has our beloved Southland been bogged down in a tragic effort to live in monologue rather than dialogue. . . .

We have waited for more than 340 years for our constitutional and God-given rights. The nations of Asia and Africa are moving with jet-like speed toward gaining political independence, but we still creep at horse-and-buggy pace toward gaining a cup of coffee at a lunch counter. Perhaps it is easy for those who have never felt the stinging darts of segregation to say, "Wait." But when you have seen vicious mobs lynch your mothers and fathers at will and drown your sisters and brothers at whim; when you have seen hate-filled policemen curse, kick and even kill your black brothers and sisters; when you see the vast majority of your twenty million Negro brothers smothering in an airtight cage of poverty in the midst of an affluent society; when you suddenly find your tongue twisted and your speech stammering as you seek to explain to your six-year-old daughter why she can't go to the public amusement park that has just been advertised on television, and see tears welling up in her eyes when she is told that Funtown is closed to colored children, and see ominous clouds of inferiority beginning to form in her little mental sky, and see her beginning to distort her personality by developing an unconscious bitterness toward white people; when you have to concoct an answer for a five-year-old son who is asking: "Daddy, why do white people treat colored people so mean?"; when you take a cross-country drive and find it necessary to sleep night after night in the uncomfortable corners of your automobile because no motel will accept you; when you are humiliated day in and day out by nagging signs reading "white" and "colored"; when your first name becomes "nigger," your middle name becomes "boy" (however old you are) and your last name becomes "John," and your wife and mother are never given the respected title "Mrs."; when you are harried by day and haunted by night by the fact that you are a Negro, living constantly at tiptoe stance, never quite knowing what to expect next, and are plagued with inner fears and outer resentments; when you are forever fighting a degenerating sense of "nobodiness"—then you will understand why we find it difficult to wait. There comes a time when the cup of endurance runs over, and men are no longer willing to be plunged into the abyss of despair. I hope, sirs, you can understand our legitimate and unavoidable impatience. . . .

I must confess that over the past few years I have been gravely disappointed with the white moderate. I have almost reached the regrettable conclusion that the Negro's great stumbling block in his stride toward freedom is not the White Citizens' Councilor or the Ku Klux Klanner, but the white moderate, who is more devoted to "order" than to justice; who prefers a negative peace which is the absence of tension to a positive peace which is the presence of justice; who constantly says: "I agree with you in the goal you seek, but I cannot agree with your methods of direct action;" who paternalistically believes he can set the timetable for another man's freedom; who lives by a mythical concept of time and who constantly advises the Negro to wait for a "more convenient season." Shallow understanding from people of good will is more frustrating than absolute misunderstanding from people of ill will. Lukewarm acceptance is much more bewildering than outright rejection.

I had hoped that the white moderate would understand that law and order exist for the purpose of establishing justice and that when they fail in this purpose they become the dangerously structured dams that block the flow of social progress. I had hoped that the white moderate would understand that the present tension in the South is a necessary phase of the transition from an obnoxious negative peace, in which the Negro passively accepted his unjust plight, to a substantive and positive peace, in which all men will respect the dignity and worth of human personality. Actually, we who engage in nonviolent direct action are not the creators of tension. We merely bring to the surface the hidden tension that is already alive. We bring it out in the open, where it can be seen and dealt with. Like a boil that can never be cured so long as it is covered up but must be opened with all its ugliness to the natural medicines of air and light, injustice must be exposed, with all the tension its exposure creates, to the light of human conscience and the air of national opinion before it can be cured. . . .

You speak of our activity in Birmingham as extreme. At first I was rather disappointed that fellow clergymen would see my nonviolent efforts as those of an extremist. I began thinking about the fact that I stand in the middle of two opposing forces in the Negro community. One is a force of complacency, made up in part of Negroes who, as a result of long years of oppression, are so drained of self-respect and a sense of "somebodiness" that they have adjusted to segregation; and in part of a few middle-class Negroes who, because of a degree of academic and economic security and because in some ways they profit by segregation, have become insensitive to the problems of the masses. The other force is one of bitterness and hatred, and it comes perilously close to advocating violence. It is expressed in the various black nationalist groups that are springing up across the nation, the largest and best-known being Elijah Muhammad's Muslim movement. Nourished by the Negro's frustration over the continued existence of racial discrimination, this movement is made up of people who have lost faith in America, who have absolutely repudiated Christianity, and who have concluded that the white man is an incorrigible "devil."

I have tried to stand between these two forces, saying that we need emulate neither the "do-nothingism" of the complacent nor the hatred and despair of the black nationalist. For there is the more excellent way of love and nonviolent protest. I am grateful to God that, through the influence of the Negro church, the way of nonviolence became an integral part of our struggle.

If this philosophy had not emerged, by now many streets of the South would, I am convinced, be flowing with blood. And I am further convinced that if our white brothers dismiss as "rabblerousers" and "outside agitators" those of us who employ nonviolent direct action, and if they refuse to support our nonviolent efforts, millions of Negroes will, out of frustration and despair, seek solace and security in black-nationalist ideologies—a development that would inevitably lead to a frightening racial nightmare.

Oppressed people cannot remain oppressed forever. The yearning for freedom eventually manifests itself, and that is what has happened to the American Negro. Something within has reminded him of his birthright of freedom, and something without has reminded him that it can be gained. Consciously or unconsciously, he has been caught up by the *Zeitgeist*, and with his black brothers of Africa and his brown and yellow brothers of Asia, South America and the Caribbean, the United States Negro is moving with a sense of great urgency toward the promised land of racial justice. If one recognizes this vital urge that has engulfed the Negro community, one should readily understand why public demonstrations are taking place. The Negro has many pent-up resentments and latent frustrations, and he must release them. So let him march; let him make prayer pilgrimages to the city hall; let him go on freedom rides—and try to understand why he must do so. If his repressed emotions are not released in nonviolent ways, they will seek expression through violence; this is not a threat but a fact of history. So I have not said to my people: "Get rid of your discontent." Rather, I have tried to say that this normal and healthy discontent can be channeled into the creative outlet of nonviolent direct action. And now this approach is being termed extremist.

But though I was initially disappointed at being categorized as an extremist, as I continued to think about the matter I gradually gained a measure of satisfaction from the label. Was not Jesus an extremist for love: "Love your enemies, bless them that curse you, do good to them that hate you, and pray for them which despitefully use you, and persecute you." Was not Amos an extremist for justice: "Let justice roll down like waters and righteousness like an ever-flowing stream." Was not Paul an extremist for the Christian gospel: "I bear in my body the marks of the Lord Jesus." Was not Martin Luther an extremist: "Here I stand; I cannot do otherwise, so help me God." And John Bunyan: "I will stay in jail to the end of my days before I make a butchery of my conscience." And Abraham Lincoln: "This nation cannot survive half slave and half free." And Thomas Jefferson: "We hold these truths to be self-evident, that all men are created equal . . . " So the question is not whether we will be extremists, but what kind of extremists we will be. Will we be extremists for hate or for love? Will we be extremists for the preservation of injustice or for the extension of justice? In that dramatic scene on Calvary's hill three men were crucified. We must never forget that all three were crucified for the same crime—the crime of extremism. Two were extremists for immorality, and thus fell below their environment. The other, Jesus Christ, was an extremist for love, truth and goodness, and thereby rose above his environment. Perhaps the South, the nation and the world are in dire need of creative extremists. . . .

Never before have I written so long a letter. I'm afraid it is much too long to take your precious time. I can assure you that it would have been much shorter if I had been writing from a comfortable desk, but what else can one do when he is alone in a narrow jail cell, other than write long letters, think long thoughts and pray long prayers?

If I have said anything in this letter that overstates the truth and indicates an unreasonable impatience, I beg you to forgive me. If I have said anything that understates the truth and indicates my having a patience that allows me to settle for anything less than brotherhood, I beg God to forgive me.

I hope this letter finds you strong in the faith. I also hope that circumstances will soon make it possible for me to meet each of you, not as an integrationist or a civil-rights leader but as a fellow clergyman and a Christian brother. Let us all hope that the dark clouds of racial prejudice will soon pass away and the deep fog of misunderstanding will be lifted from our fear-drenched communities, and in some not too distant tomorrow the radiant stars of love and brotherhood will shine over our great nation with all their scintillating beauty.

Yours for the cause of Peace and Brotherhood,
MARTIN LUTHER KING, JR.

DOCUMENT NO. 8

JOHN KENNEDY SPEAKS ON CIVIL RIGHTS
JUNE 11, 1963*

On the afternoon of June 11, 1963 Governor of Alabama George Wallace kept his promise to "stand in the schoolhouse door" at the University of Alabama in an attempt to avoid desegregation of that university. Violence was averted, and the university was desegregated. That evening, President Kennedy spoke to the nation on the issue of race.

γ   γ   γ

Good evening, my fellow citizens:

This afternoon, following a series of threats and defiant statements, the presence of Alabama National Guardsmen was required on the University of Alabama campus to carry out the final and unequivocal order of the United States District Court of the Northern District of Alabama. That order called for the admission of two clearly qualified young Alabama residents who happened to have been born Negro.

That they were admitted peacefully on the campus is due in good measure to the conduct of the students of the University of Alabama, who met their responsibilities in a constructive way.

I hope that every American, regardless of where he lives, will stop and examine his conscience about this and other related incidents. This Nation was founded by men of many nations and backgrounds. It was founded on the principle that all men are created equal, and that the rights of every man are diminished when the rights of one man are threatened.

Today we are committed to a worldwide struggle to promote and protect the rights of all who wish to be free. And when Americans are sent to Viet-Nam or West Berlin, we do not ask for whites only. It ought to be possible, therefore, for American students of any color to attend any public institution they select without having to be backed up by troops.

It ought to be possible for American consumers of any color to receive equal service in places of public accommodation, such as hotels and res-

*Source: *Public Papers of the Presidents of the United States, John F. Kennedy*, vol. 3, 1963, pp. 468–71.

taurants and theaters and retail stores, without being forced to resort to demonstrations in the street, and it ought to be possible for American citizens of any color to register and to vote in a free election without interference or fear of reprisal.

It ought to be possible, in short, for every American to enjoy the privileges of being American without regard to his race or his color. In short, every American ought to have the right to be treated as he would wish to be treated, as one would wish his children to be treated. But this is not the case.

The Negro baby born in America today, regardless of the section of the Nation in which he is born, has about one-half as much chance of completing a high school as a white baby born in the same place on the same day, one-third as much chance of completing college, one-third as much chance of becoming a professional man, twice as much chance of becoming unemployed, about one-seventh as much chance of earning $10,000 a year, a life expectancy which is 7 years shorter, and the prospects of earning only half as much.

This is not a sectional issue. Difficulties over segregation and discrimination exist in every city, in every State of the Union, producing in many cities a rising tide of discontent that threatens the public safety. Nor is this a partisan issue. In a time of domestic crisis men of good will and generosity should be able to unite regardless of party or politics. This is not even a legal or legislative issue alone. It is better to settle these matters in the courts than on the streets, and new laws are needed at every level, but law alone cannot make men see right.

We are confronted primarily with a moral issue. It is as old as the scriptures and is as clear as the American Constitution.

The heart of the question is whether all Americans are to be afforded equal rights and equal opportunities, whether we are going to treat our fellow Americans as we want to be treated. If an American, because his skin is dark, cannot eat lunch in a restaurant open to the public, if he cannot send his children to the best public school available, if he cannot vote for the public officials who represent him, if, in short, he cannot enjoy the full and free life which all of us want, then who among us would be content to have the color of his skin changed and stand in his place? Who among us would then be content with the counsels of patience and delay?

One hundred years of delay have passed since President Lincoln freed the slaves, yet their heirs, their grandsons, are not fully free. They are not yet freed from the bonds of injustice. They are not yet freed from social and economic oppression. And this Nation, for all its hopes and all its boasts, will not be fully free until all its citizens are free.

We preach freedom around the world, and we mean it, and we cherish our freedom here at home, but are we to say to the world, and much more importantly, to each other that this is a land of the free except for the Negroes; that we have no second-class citizens except Negroes; that we have no class or cast system, no ghettoes, no master race except with respect to Negroes?

Now the time has come for this Nation to fulfill its promise. The events in Birmingham and elsewhere have so increased the cries for equality that no city or State or legislative body can prudently choose to ignore them.

The fires of frustration and discord are burning in every city, North and South, where legal remedies are not at hand. Redress is sought in the streets, in demonstrations, parades, and protests which create tensions and threaten violence and threaten lives.

We face, therefore, a moral crisis as a country and as a people. It cannot be met by repressive police action. It cannot be left to increased demonstrations in the streets. It cannot be quieted by token moves or talk. It is a time to act in the Congress, in your State and local legislative body and, above all, in all of our daily lives.

It is not enough to pin the blame on others, to say this is a problem of one section of the country or another, or deplore the fact that we face. A great change is at hand, and our task, our obligation, is to make that revolution, that change, peaceful and constructive for all.

Those who do nothing are inviting shame as well as violence. Those who act boldly are recognizing right as well as reality.

Next week I shall ask the Congress of the United States to act, to make a commitment it has not fully made in this century to the proposition that race has no place in American life or law. The Federal judiciary has upheld that proposition in a series of forthright cases. The executive branch has adopted that proposition in the conduct of its affairs, including the employment of Federal personnel, the use of Federal facilities, and the sale of federally financed housing.

But there are other necessary measures which only the Congress can provide, and they must be provided at this session. The old code of equity law under which we live commands for every wrong a remedy, but in too many communities, in too many parts of the country, wrongs are inflicted on Negro citizens and there are no remedies at law. Unless the Congress acts, their only remedy is in the street.

I am, therefore, asking the Congress to enact legislation giving all Americans the right to be served in facilities which are open to the public—hotels, restaurants, theaters, retail stores, and similar establishments.

This seems to me to be an elementary right. Its denial is an arbitrary indignity that no American in 1963 should have to endure, but many do.

I have recently met with scores of business leaders urging them to take voluntary action to end this discrimination and I have been encouraged by their response, and in the last 2 weeks over 75 cities have seen progress made in desegregating these kinds of facilities. But many are unwilling to act alone, and for this reason, nationwide legislation is needed if we are to move this problem from the streets to the courts.

I am also asking Congress to authorize the Federal Government to participate more fully in lawsuits designed to end segregation in public education. We have succeeded in persuading many districts to desegregate voluntarily. Dozens have admitted Negroes without violence. Today a Negro is attending a State-supported institution in every one of our 50 States, but the pace is very slow.

Too many Negro children entering segregated grade schools at the time of the Supreme Court's decision 9 years ago will enter segregated high schools this fall, having suffered a loss which can never be restored. The lack of an adequate education denies the Negro a chance to get a decent job.

The orderly implementation of the Supreme Court decision, therefore, cannot be left solely to those who may not have the economic resources to carry the legal action or who may be subject to harassment.

Other features will be also requested, including greater protection for the right to vote. But legislation, I repeat, cannot solve this problem alone. It must be solved in the homes of every American in every community across our country.

In this respect, I want to pay tribute to those citizens North and South who have been working in their communities to make life better for all. They are acting not out of a sense of legal duty but out of a sense of human decency.

Like our soldiers and sailors in all parts of the world they are meeting freedom's challenge on the firing line, and I salute them for their honor and their courage.

My fellow Americans, this is a problem which faces us all—in every city of the North as well as the South. Today there are Negroes unemployed, two or three times as many compared to whites, inadequate in education, moving into the large cities, unable to find work, young people particularly out of work without hope, denied equal rights, denied the opportunity to eat at a restaurant or lunch counter or go to a movie theater, denied the right to a decent education, denied almost today the right to attend a State university even though qualified. It seems to me that these are matters which concern us all, not merely Presidents or Congressmen or Governors, but every citizen of the United States.

This is one country. It has become one country because all of us and all the people who came here had an equal chance to develop their talents.

We cannot say to 10 percent of the population that you can't have that right; that your children can't have the chance to develop whatever talents they have; that the only way that they are going to get their rights is to go into the streets and demonstrate. I think we owe them and we owe ourselves a better country than that.

Therefore, I am asking for your help in making it easier for us to move ahead and to provide the kind of equality of treatment which we would want ourselves; to give a chance for every child to be educated to the limit of his talents.

As I have said before, not every child has an equal talent or an equal ability or an equal motivation, but they should have the equal right to develop their talent and their ability and their motivation, to make something of themselves.

We have a right to expect that the Negro community will be responsible, will uphold the law, but they have a right to expect that the law will be fair, that the Constitution will be color blind, as Justice Harlan said at the turn of the century.

This is what we are talking about and this is a matter which concerns this country and what it stands for, and in meeting it I ask the support of all our citizens.

Thank you very much.

DOCUMENT NO. 9

"I HAVE A DREAM"
WASHINGTON, D.C., AUGUST 28, 1963*

On August 28, 1963, the civil rights movement reached its apex at the March on Washington, a celebration of the successes of the movement. The march was also intended to pressure Congress to pass the administration-sponsored civil rights bill. The crowning event of the March on Washington was King's "I have a dream" speech. As Harvard Sitkoff has written, King's speech "transformed an amiable effort at lobbying Congress into scintillating historic event."

γ   γ   γ

Five score years ago, a great American, in whose symbolic shadow we stand, signed the Emancipation Proclamation. This momentous decree came as a great beacon light of hope to millions of Negro slaves who had been seared in the flames of withering injustice. It came as a joyous daybreak to end the long night of captivity.

But one hundred years later, we must face the tragic fact that the Negro is still not free. One hundred years later, the life of the Negro is still sadly crippled by the manacles of segregation and the chains of discrimination. One hundred years later, the Negro lives on a lonely island of poverty in the midst of a vast ocean of material prosperity. One hundred years later, the Negro is still languished in the corners of American society and finds himself an exile in his own land. So we have come here today to dramatize an appalling condition.

In a sense we have come to our nation's Capitol to cash a check. When the architects of our republic wrote the magnificent words of the Constitution and the Declaration of Independence, they were signing a promissory note to which every American was to fall heir. This note was a promise that all men would be guaranteed the unalienable rights of life, liberty, and the pursuit of happiness.

It is obvious today that America has defaulted on this promissory note insofar as her citizens of color are concerned. Instead of honoring this sacred obligation, America has given the Negro people a bad check; a check which has come back marked "insufficient funds." But we refuse to believe that the bank of justice is bankrupt. We refuse to believe that there are insufficient funds in the great vaults of opportunity of this nation. So we have come to cash this check—a check that will give us upon demand the riches of freedom and the security of justice. We have also come to this hallowed spot to remind America of the fierce urgency of *now*. This is no time to engage in the luxury of cooling off or to take the tranquilizing drug of gradualism. *Now* is the time to make real the promises of Democracy. *Now* is the time to rise from the dark and desolate valley of segregation to the sunlit path of racial justice. *Now* is the time to open the doors of opportunity to all of God's children. *Now* is the time to lift our nation from the quicksands of racial injustice to the solid rock of brotherhood.

It would be fatal for the nation to overlook the urgency of the moment and to underestimate the determination of the Negro. This sweltering summer of the Negro's legitimate discontent will not pass until there is an invigorating autumn of freedom and equality. 1963 is not an end, but a beginning. Those who hope that the Negro needed to blow off steam and will now be content will have a rude awakening if the Nation returns to business as usual. There will be neither rest nor tranquility in America until the Negro is granted his citizenship rights. The whirlwinds of revolt will continue to shake the foundations of our Nation until the bright day of justice emerges.

But there is something that I must say to my people who stand on the warm threshold which leads into the palace of justice. In the process of gaining our rightful place we must not be guilty of wrongful deeds. Let us not seek to satisfy our thirst for freedom by drinking from the cup of bitterness and hatred.

We must forever conduct our struggle on the high plane of dignity and discipline. We must not allow our creative protest to degenerate into physical violence. Again and again we must rise to the majestic heights of meeting physical force with soul force. The marvelous new militancy which has engulfed the Negro community must not lead us to a distrust of all white people, for many of our white brothers, as evidenced by their presence here today, have come to realize that their destiny is tied up with our destiny and their freedom is inextricably bound to our freedom. We cannot walk alone.

And as we walk, we must make the pledge that we shall march ahead. We cannot turn back. There are those who are asking the devotees of civil rights, "when will you be satisfied?" We can never be satisfied as long as the Negro is the victim of the unspeakable horrors of police brutality. We can never be satisfied as long as our bodies, heavy with the fatigue of travel, cannot gain lodging in the motels of the highways and the hotels of the cities. We cannot be satisfied as long as the Negro's basic mobility is from a smaller ghetto to a larger one. We can never be satisfied as long as a Negro in Mississippi cannot vote and a Negro in New York believes he has nothing for which to vote. No, no we are not satisfied, and we will not be satisfied until justice rolls down like waters and righteousness like a mighty stream.

I am not unmindful that some of you have come here out of great trials and tribulations. Some of you have come fresh from narrow jail cells. Some of you have come from areas where your quest for freedom left you battered by the storms of persecution and staggered by the winds of police brutality. You have been the veterans of creative suffering. Continue to work with the faith that unearned suffering is redemptive.

Go back to Mississippi, go back to Alabama, go back to South Carolina, go back to Georgia, go back to Louisiana, go back to the slums and ghettos of our northern cities, knowing that somehow this situation can and will be changed. Let us not wallow in the valley of despair.

I say to you today, my friends, that in spite of the difficulties and frustrations of the moment I still have a dream. It is a dream deeply rooted in the American dream.

I have a dream that one day this nation will rise up and live out the true meaning of its creed: "We hold these truths to be self-evident; that all men are created equal."

I have a dream that one day on the red hills of Georgia the sons of former slaves and the sons of former slaveowners will be able to sit down together at the table of brotherhood.

I have a dream that one day even the state of Mississippi, a desert state sweltering with the heat of injustice and oppression, will be transformed into an oasis of freedom and justice.

I have a dream that my four little children will one day live in a nation where they will not be judged by the color of their skin but by the content of their character.

I have a dream today.

I have a dream that one day the state of Alabama, whose governor's lips are presently dripping with the words of interposition and nullification, will be transformed into a situation where little black boys and black girls will be able to join hands with little white boys and white girls and walk together as sisters and brothers.

I have a dream today.

I have a dream that one day every valley shall be exalted, every hill and mountain shall be made low, the rough places will be made plains, and the crooked places will be made straight, and the glory of the Lord shall be revealed, and all flesh shall see it together.

This is our hope. This is the faith with which I return to the South. With this faith we will be able to hew out of the mountain of despair a stone of hope. With this faith we will be able to transform the jangling discords of our nation into a beautiful symphony of brotherhood. With this faith we will be able to work together, to pray together, to struggle together, to go to jail together, to stand up for freedom together, knowing that we will be free one day.

This will be the day when all of God's children will be able to sing with new meaning "My country 'tis of thee, sweet land of liberty, of thee I sing. Land where my fathers died, land of the pilgrim's pride, from every mountainside, let freedom ring."

And if America is to be a great nation this must become true. So let freedom ring from the prodigious hilltops of New Hampshire. Let freedom ring from the mighty mountains of New York. Let freedom ring from the heightening Alleghenies of Pennsylvania!

Let freedom ring from the snowcapped Rockies of Colorado!

Let freedom ring from the curvaceous peaks of California!

But not only that; let freedom ring from Stone Mountain of Georgia!

Let freedom ring from Lookout Mountain of Tennessee!

Let freedom ring from every hill and mole hill of Mississippi. From every mountainside, let freedom ring.

When we let freedom ring, when we let it ring from every village and every hamlet, from every state and every city, we will be able to speed up that day when all of God's children, black men and white men, Jews and Gentiles, Protestants and Catholics, will be able to join hands and sing in the words of the old Negro spiritual, "Free at last! free at last! thank God almighty, we are free at last!"

DOCUMENT NO. 10

FANNIE LOU HAMER SPEAKS FOR THE MISSISSIPPI FREEDOM DEMOCRATIC PARTY ATLANTIC CITY, 1964*

In the summer of 1964 the Mississippi Democratic Party sent an all-white delegation to the Democratic National Convention in Atlantic City. In response the integrated Mississippi Freedom Democratic Party (MFDP) was formed (mostly out of the leadership of the Student Nonviolent Coordinating Committee) and attempted to unseat the all-white Mississippi delegation. One of the primary leaders of the MFDP was Fannie Lou Hamer, a former Mississippi sharecropper. Her address before the party's credentials committee threatened to embarrass President Lyndon Johnson who wanted the convention to be a platform for his accomplishments and campaign promises. The president called a press conference to keep Hamer's speech, which follows here, from being broadcast on national television.

γ   γ   γ

Mr. Chairman, and the Credentials Committee, my name is Mrs. Fannie Lou Hamer, and I live at 626 East Lafayette Street, Ruleville, Mississippi, Sunflower County, the home of Senator James O. Eastland, and Senator Stennis.

It was the 31st of August in 1962 that eighteen of us traveled twenty-six miles to the county courthouse in Indianola to try to register to try to become first-class citizens. We was met in Indianola by Mississippi men, highway patrolmens, and they only allowed two of us in to take the literacy test at the time. After we had taken this test and started back to Ruleville, we was held up by the City Police and the State Highway Patrolmen and carried back to Indianola, where the bus driver was charged that day with driving a bus the wrong color.

After we paid the fine among us, we continued on to Ruleville, and Reverend Jeff Sunny carried me four miles in the rural area where I had worked as a timekeeper and sharecropper for eighteen years. I was met there by my children, who told me the plantation owner was angry because I had gone down to try to register. After they told me, my husband

*Source: Kay Mills, *This Little Light of Mine* New York, 1993.

came, and said the plantation owner was raising cain because I had tried to register, and before he quit talking the plantation owner came, and said, "Fannie Lou, do you know—did Pap tell you what I said?"

I said, "Yes, sir."

He said, "I mean that," he said. "If you don't go down and withdraw your registration, you will have to leave," said, "Then if you go down and withdraw," he said. "You will—you might have to go because we are not ready for that in Mississippi."

And I addressed him and told him and said, "I didn't try to register for you. I tried to register for myself." I had to leave that same night.

On the 10th of September, 1962, sixteen bullets was fired into the home of Mr. and Mrs. Robert Tucker for me. That same night two girls were shot in Ruleville, Mississippi. Also Mr. Joe McDonald's house was shot in.

And in June the 9th, 1963, I had attended a voter-registration workshop, was returning back to Mississippi. Ten of us was traveling by the Continental Trailway bus. When we got to Winona, Mississippi, which is Montgomery County, four of the people got off to use the washroom, and two of the people—to use the restaurant—two of the people wanted to use the washroom. The four people that had gone in to use the restaurant was ordered out. During this time I was on the bus. But when I looked through the window and saw they had rushed out, I got off of the bus to see what had happened, and one of the ladies said, "It was a state highway patrolman and a chief of police ordered us out."

I got back on the bus and one of the persons had used the washroom got back on the bus, too. As soon as I was seated on the bus, I saw when they began to get the four people in a highway patrolman's car. I stepped off the bus to see what was happening and somebody screamed from the car that the four workers was in and said, "Get that one there," and when I went to get in the car, when the man told me I was under arrest, he kicked me.

I was carried to the county jail, and put in the booking room. They left some of the people in the booking room and began to place us in cells. I was placed in a cell with a young woman called Miss Euvester Simpson. After I was placed in the cell I began to hear sounds of licks and screams. I could hear the sounds of licks and horrible screams, and I could hear somebody say, "Can you say, yes sir, nigger? Can you say yes, sir?"

And they would say other horrible names. She would say, "Yes, I can say yes, sir."

"So say it."

She says, "I don't know you well enough."

They beat her, I don't know how long, and after a while she began to pray, and asked God to have mercy on those people.

And it wasn't too long before three white men came to my cell. One of these men was a State Highway Patrolman and he asked me where I was from, and I told him Ruleville. He said, "We are going to check this." And they left my cell and it wasn't too long before they came back. He said "You are from Ruleville all right," and he used a curse word, and he said, "We are going to make you wish you was dead."

I was carried out of that cell into another cell where they had two Negro prisoners. The State Highway Patrolman ordered the first Negro to take the blackjack. The first Negro prisoner ordered me, by orders from the State Highway Patrolman for me, to lay down on a bunk bed on my face, and I laid on my face. The first Negro began to beat, and I was beat by the first Negro until he was exhausted, and I was holding my hands behind me at that time on my left side because I suffered from polio when I was six years old. After the first Negro had beat until he was exhausted, the State Highway Patrolman ordered the second Negro to take the blackjack.

The second Negro began to beat and I began to work my feet, and the State Highway Patrolman ordered the first Negro who had beat to set on my feet to keep me from working my feet. I began to scream and one white man got up and began to beat me in my head and tell me to hush. One white man—my dress had worked up high, he walked over and pulled my dress down—and he pulled my dress back, back up.

I was in jail when Medgar Evers was murdered. . . .

All of this is on account we want to register, to become first-class citizens, and if the Freedom Democratic Party is not seated now, I question America, is this America, the land of the free and the home of the brave where we have to sleep with our telephones off the hooks because our lives be threatened daily because we want to live as decent human beings, in America?

"Thank you."

DOCUMENT NO. 11

LYNDON JOHNSON'S SPECIAL MESSAGE TO CONGRESS MARCH 15, 1965*

On March 15, 1965, just one week after the brutal attack on black marchers by Alabama state officials and Selma police, Lyndon Johnson addressed the nation and placed the full weight of the presidency behind voting rights legislation.

γ   γ   γ

I speak tonight for the dignity of man and the destiny of democracy.

I urge every member of both parties, Americans of all religions and of all colors, from every section of this country, to join me in that cause.

At times history and fate meet at a single time in a single place to shape a turning point in man's unending search for freedom. So it was at Lexington and Concord. So it was a century ago at Appomattox. So it was last week in Selma, Alabama. There, long-suffering men and women peacefully protested the denial of their rights as Americans. Many were brutally assaulted. One good man, a man of God, was killed. There is no cause for pride in what has happened in Selma. There is no cause for self-satisfaction in the long denial of equal rights of millions of Americans. But there is cause for hope and for faith in our democracy in what is happening here tonight. For the cries of pain and the hymns and protests of oppressed people, have summoned into convocation all the majesty of this great government of the greatest nation on earth.

Our mission is at once the oldest and the most basic of this country: to right wrong, to do justice, to serve man. . . . Rarely in any time does an issue lay bare the secret heart of America itself. Rarely are we met with a challenge, not to our growth or abundance, or our welfare or our security, but rather to the values and the purposes and the meaning of our beloved nation.

The issue of equal rights for American Negroes is such an issue. And should we defeat every enemy, and should we double our wealth and

*Source: *Public Papers of the Presidents of the United State: LBJ, 1965*, Vol. 1, pp. 281–87.

conquer the stars and still be unequal to this issue, then we will have failed as a people and as a nation.

For with a country as with a person, "What is a man profited, if he shall gain the whole world, and lose his own soul?"

There is no Negro problem. There is no Southern problem. There is no Northern problem. There is only an American problem. And we are met here tonight as Americans, not as Democrats or Republicans, we are met here as Americans to solve that problem.

This was the first nation in the history of the world to be founded with a purpose. The great phrases of that purpose still sound in every American heart, North and South: "All men are created equal"—"government by consent of the governed"—"give me liberty or give me death." Those are not just clever words. Those are not just empty theories. In their name Americans have fought and died for two centuries, and tonight around the world they stand there as guardians of our liberty, risking their lives.

Those words are a promise to every citizen that he shall share in the dignity of man. This dignity cannot be found in a man's possessions. It cannot be found in his power or in his position. It really rests on his right to be treated as a man equal in opportunity to all others. It says that he shall share in freedom, he shall choose his leaders, educate his children, provide for his family according to his ability and his merits as a human being.

To apply any other test—to deny a man his hopes because of his color or race, or his religion, or the place of his birth—is not only to do injustice, it is to deny America and to dishonor the dead who gave their lives for American freedom.

Our fathers believed that if this noble view of the rights of man was to flourish, it must be rooted in democracy. The most basic right of all was the right to choose your own leaders. The history of this country in large measure is the history of expansion of that right to all of our people.

Many of the issues of civil rights are very complex and most difficult. But about this there can and should be no argument. Every American citizen must have an equal right to vote. There is no reason which can excuse the denial of that right. There is no duty which weighs more heavily on us than the duty we have to ensure that right.

Yet the harsh fact is that in many places in this country men and women are kept from voting simply because they are Negroes.

Every device of which human ingenuity is capable has been used to deny this right. The Negro citizen may go to register only to be told that the day is wrong, or the hour is late, or the official in charge is absent. And if he persists and if he manages to present himself to the registrar, he may be disqualified because he did not spell out his middle name or because he abbreviated a word on the application. And if he manages to fill out an application he is given a test. The registrar is the sole judge of whether he passes this test. He may be asked to recite the entire constitution, or explain the most complex provisions of state laws. And even a college degree cannot be used to prove that he can read and write.

For the fact is that the only way to pass these barriers is to show a white skin.

Experience has clearly shown that the existing process of law cannot overcome systematic and ingenious discrimination. No law that we now have on the books—and I have helped to put three of them there—can ensure the right to vote when local officials are determined to deny it.

In such a case our duty must be clear to all of us. The Constitution says that no person shall be kept from voting because of his race or his color. We have all sworn on oath before God to support and to defend that Constitution. We must now act in obedience to that oath.

Wednesday I will send to Congress a law designed to eliminate illegal barriers to the right to vote. . . .

This bill will strike down restrictions to voting in all elections—Federal, State, and local—which have been used to deny Negroes the right to vote. This bill will establish a simple, uniform standard which cannot be used, however ingenious the effort, to flout our Constitution. It will provide for citizens to be registered by officials of the United States government if the State officials refuse to register them. It will eliminate tedious, unnecessary lawsuits which delay the right to vote. Finally, this legislation will ensure that properly registered individuals are not prohibited from voting. . . .

There is no constitutional issue here. The command of the Constitution is plain.

There is no moral issue. It is wrong to deny any of your fellow Americans the right to vote in this country.

There is no issue of states rights or national rights. There is only the struggle for human rights.

I have not the slightest doubt what will be your answer.

But the last time a President sent a civil rights bill to the Congress it contained a provision to protect voting rights in Federal elections. That civil rights bill was passed after eight long months of debate. And when that bill came to my desk from the Congress for my signature, the heart of the voting provision had been eliminated.

This time, on this issue, there must be no delay, or no hesitation or no compromise with our purpose.

We cannot, we must not refuse to protect the right of every American to vote in every election that he may desire to participate in. . . .

Even if we pass this bill, the battle will not be over. What happened in Selma is part of a far larger movement which reaches into every section and state of America. It is the effort of American Negroes to secure for themselves the full blessings of American life.

Their cause must be our cause too. Because it is not just Negroes, but really it is all of us, who must overcome the crippling legacy of bigotry and injustice. And we shall overcome.

As a man whose roots go deeply into Southern soil I know how agonizing racial feelings are. I know how difficult it is to reshape the attitudes and the structure of our society.

But a century has passed, more than a hundred years, since the Negro was freed. And he is not fully free tonight.

It was more than a hundred years ago that Abraham Lincoln, the great President of the Northern party, signed the Emancipation Proclamation, but emancipation is a proclamation and not a fact.

A century has passed, more than a hundred years since equality was promised. And yet the Negro is not equal.

A century has passed since the day of promise. And the promise is unkept.

The time of justice has now come. I tell you that I believe sincerely that no force can hold it back. It is right in the eyes of man and God that it should come. And when it does, I think that day will brighten the lives of every American.

For Negroes are not the only victims. How many white children have gone uneducated, how many white families have lived in stark poverty, how many white lives have been scarred by fear because we wasted our energy and our substance to maintain the barriers of hatred and terror.

So I say to all of you here and to all in the nation tonight, that those who appeal to you to hold on to the past do so at the cost of denying you your future.

This great, rich, restless country can offer opportunity and education and hope to all—all black and white, all North and South, sharecropper, and city dweller. These are the enemies—poverty, ignorance, disease. They are enemies, not our fellow man, not our neighbor, and these enemies too, poverty, disease and ignorance, we shall overcome.

Now let none of us in any section look with prideful righteousness on the troubles in another section or the problems of our neighbors. There is really no part of America where the promise of equality has been fully kept. In Buffalo as well as in Birmingham, in Philadelphia as well as in Selma, Americans are struggling for the fruits of freedom.

This is one nation. What happens in Selma or in Cincinnati is a matter of legitimate concern to every American. But let each of us look within our own hearts and our own communities, and let each of us put our shoulder to the wheel to root out injustice wherever it exists.

The real hero of this struggle is the American Negro. His actions and protests, his courage to risk safety and even to risk his life, have awakened the conscience of this nation. His demonstrations have been designed to call attention to injustice, designed to provoke change, designed to stir reform. He has called upon us to make good the promise of America. And who among us can say that we would have made the same progress were it not for his persistent bravery, and his faith in American democracy.

DOCUMENT NO. 12

CHARLES HAMILTON DEFINES BLACK POWER*

Charles Hamilton, along with Stokely Carmichael, attempted several times to define black power, a phrase that became more and more abstract as the decade of the 1960s drew to an end. The essay below is another attempt by Hamilton to define black power. He begins his essay by explaining the difficulty of the endeavor.

γ   γ   γ

Black Power has many definitions and connotations in the rhetoric of race relations today. To some people, it is synonymous with premeditated acts of violence to destroy the political and economic institutions of this country. Others equate Black Power with plans to rid the civil-rights movement of whites who have been in it for years. The concept is understood by many to mean hatred of and separation from whites; it is associated with calling whites "honkies" and with shouts of "Burn, baby, burn!" Some understand it to be the use of pressure-group tactics in the accepted tradition of the American political process. And still others say that Black Power must be seen first of all as an attempt to instill a sense of identity and pride in black people.

Ultimately, I suspect, we have to accept the fact that, in this highly charged atmosphere, it is virtually impossible to come up with a single definition satisfactory to all.

Even as some of us try to articulate our idea of Black Power and the way we relate to it and advocate it, we are categorized as "moderate" or "militant" or "reasonable" or "extremist." "I can accept your definition of Black Power," a listener will say to me. "But how does your position compare with what Stokely Carmichael said in Cuba or with what H. Rap Brown said in Cambridge, Md.?" Or, just as frequently, some young white New Left advocate will come up to me and proudly announce: "You're not radical enough. Watts, Newark, Detroit—that's what's happening, man! You're nothing but a reformist. We've got to blow up this society. Read Che or Debray or Mao." All I can do is shrug

*Source: *New York Times Magazine*, April 14, 1968

113

and conclude that some people believe that making a revolution in this country involves rhetoric, Molotov cocktails and being under 30.

To have Black Power equated with calculated acts of violence would be very unfortunate. First, if black people have learned anything over the years, it is that he who shouts revolution the loudest is one of the first to run when the action starts. Second, open calls to violence are a sure way to have one's ranks immediately infiltrated. Third—and this is as important as any reason—violent revolution in this country would fail; it would be met with the kind of repression used in Sharpeville, South Africa, in 1960, when 67 Africans were killed and 186 wounded during a demonstration against apartheid. It is clear that America is not above this. There are many white bigots who would like nothing better than to embark on a program of black genocide, even though the imposition of such repressive measures would destroy civil liberties for whites as well as for blacks. Some whites are so panicky, irrational and filled with racial hatred that they would welcome the opportunity to annihilate the black community. This was clearly shown in the senseless murder of Dr. Martin Luther King Jr., which understandably—but nonetheless irrationally—prompted some black militants to advocate violent retaliation. Such cries for revenge intensify racial fear and animosity when the need—now more than ever—is to establish solid, stable organizations and action programs.

Many whites will take comfort in these words of caution against violence. But they should not. The truth is that the black ghettos are going to continue to blow up out of sheer frustration and rage, and no amount of rhetoric from professors writing articles in magazines (which most black people in the ghettos do not read anyway) will affect that. There comes a point beyond which people cannot be expected to endure prejudice, oppression and deprivation, and they *will* explode. . . .

Black Power rejects the lessons of slavery and segregation that caused black people to look upon themselves with hatred and disdain. To be "integrated" it was necessary to deny one's heritage, one's own culture, to be ashamed of one's black skin, thick lips and kinky hair. In their book, "Racial Crisis in America," two Florida State University sociologists, Lewis M. Killian and Charles M. Grigg, wrote: "At the present time, integration as a solution to the race problem demands that the Negro forswear his identity as a Negro. But for a lasting solution, the meaning of 'American' must lose its implicit racial modifier, 'white.' " The black man must change his demeaning conception of himself; he must develop a sense of pride and self-respect. Then, if integration comes, it will deal with people who are psychologically and mentally healthy, with people who have a sense of their history and of themselves as whole human beings. . . .

This brings us to a consideration of the external problems of the black community. It is clear that black people will need the help of whites at many places along the line. There simply are not sufficient economic resources—actual or potential—in the black community for a total, unilateral, boot-strap operation. Why should there be? Black people have been the target of deliberate denial for centuries, and racist America has done its job well. This is a serious problem that must be faced by Black Power advocates. On the one hand, they recognize the need to be independent of "the white power structure." And on the other, they must frequently turn to that structure for help—technical and financial. Thus, the rhetoric and the reality often clash.

Resolution probably lies in the realization by white America that it is in her interest not to have a weak, dependent, alienated black community inhabiting the inner cities and blowing them up periodically. Society needs stability, and as long as there is a sizable powerless, restless group within it which considers the society illegitimate, stability is not possible. However it is calculated, the situation calls for a black-white rapprochement, which may well come only through additional confrontations and crises. More frequently than not, the self-interest of the dominant society is not clearly perceived until the brink is reached.

DOCUMENT NO. 13

ROY WILKINS AND THE NAACP'S
OPPOSITION TO BLACK POWER
JULY 5, 1966*

Roy Wilkins served as the NAACP's executive director from 1955 to 1977. He was one of several prominent black leaders who opposed the shift toward black power in the civil rights movement. Here, as he addresses the 57th annual meeting of the NAACP, he lashes out at black power.

γ γ γ

All about us are alarms and confusions as well as great and challenging developments. Differences of opinion are sharper. For the first time since several organizations began to function where only two had functioned before, there emerges what seems to be a difference in goals.

Heretofore there were some differences in methods and emphasis but none in ultimate goals. The end was always to be the inclusion of the American Negro, without racial discrimination, as a full-fledged equal in all phases of American citizenship.

There has now emerged, first a strident and threatening challenge to a strategy widely employed by civil rights groups, namely nonviolence. One organization which has been meeting in Baltimore has passed a resolution declaring for defense of themselves by Negro citizens if they are attacked.

This position is not new as far as the N.A.A.C.P. is concerned. Historically our association has defended in court those persons who have defended themselves and their homes with firearms.

But neither have we couched a policy of manly resistance in such a way that our members and supporters felt compelled to maintain themselves in an armed state, ready to retaliate instantly and in kind whenever attacked.

Sees 'Counterviolence'

We venture the observation that such a publicized posture could serve to stir counter-planning, counteraction and possible conflict. If carried

*SOURCE: New York Times (July 6, 1966)

out literally as instant retaliation in cases adjudged by aggrieved persons to have been grossly unjust, this policy could produce—in extreme situations—lynchings, or, in better-sounding phraseology, private vigilante vengeance.

Moreover, in attempting to substitute for derelict law enforcement machinery, the policy entails the risk of a broader, more indiscriminate crack-down by law officers under the ready-made excuse of restoring law and order.

It seems reasonable to assume that proclaimed protective violence is as likely to encourage counterviolence as it is to discourage violent persecution.

But the more serious division in the civil rights movement is the one posed by a word formulation that implied clearly a difference in goals.

No matter how endlessly they try to explain it, the term "black power" means antiwhite power. In a racially pluralistic society, the concept, the formation and the exercise of that ethnically tagged power means opposition to other ethnic powers. In the black-white relationship, it has to mean that every other ethnic power is the rival and the antagonist of "black power." It has to mean "going it alone." It has to mean separatism.

Now, separatism, whether on the rarefied debate level of "black power" or on the wishful level of a Secessionist Freedom City in Watts, offers a disadvantaged minority little except a chance to shrivel and die.

Ideologically it dictates "up with black and down with white" in precisely the same manner that South Africa reverses that slogan.

It is a reverse Mississippi, a reverse Hitler, a reverse Ku Klux Klan.

If these were evil in our judgment, what virtue can we claim for black over white. If, as some proponents claim, this concept instills pride of race, cannot this pride be taught without preaching hatred or supremacy based on race?

We of the N.A.A.C.P. will have none of this. We have fought it too long. It is the ranging of race against race on the irrelevant basis of skin color. It is the father of hatred and the mother of violence.

It is the wicked fanaticism which has swelled out tears, broken our bodies, squeezed our hearts and taken the blood of our black and white loved ones. It shall not now poison our forward march.

We seek therefore, as we have sought these many years, for the inclusion of Negro Americans in the nation's life, not their exclusion. This is our land, as much as it is any American's—every square foot of every city and town and village. The task of winning our share is not the easy one of disengagement and flight, but the hard one of work, of short as well as long jumps, of disappointments and of sweet success.

DOCUMENT NO. 14

ELDRIDGE CLEAVER ON WATTS*

In his book Soul on Ice, *Eldridge Cleaver writes of his time in California's Folsom Prison, where he served nine years for rape. Here he recalls the reaction black inmates displayed during the Watts riots in Los Angeles. Cleaver held several posts in the Black Panthers, including minister of culture, minister of education, and field marshall. In 1968 Cleaver ran for president on the Peace and Freedom Party and won nearly 200,000 votes. "The Preacher" that he refers to in the following excerpt is Martin Luther King.*

γ   γ   γ

As we left the Mess Hall Sunday morning and milled around in the prison yard, after four days of abortive uprising in Watts, a group of low riders from Watts assembled on the basketball court. They were wearing jubilant, triumphant smiles, animated by a vicarious spirit by which they, too, were in the thick of the uprising taking place hundreds of miles away to the south in the Watts ghetto.

"Man," said one, "what they doing out there? Break it down for me, Baby."

They slapped each other's outstretched palms in a cool salute and burst out laughing with joy.

"Home boy, them Brothers is taking care of Business!" shrieked another ecstatically.

Then one low rider, stepping into the center of the circle formed by the others, reared back on his legs and swaggered, hunching his belt up with his forearms as he'd seen James Cagney and George Raft do in too many gangster movies. I joined the circle. Sensing a creative moment in the offing, we all got very quiet, very still, and others passing by joined the circle and did likewise.

"Baby," he said, "They walking in fours and kicking in doors, dropping Reds and busting heads; drinking wine and committing crime, shooting and looting; high-siding and low-riding, setting fires and slashing tires; turning over cars and burning down bars; making Parker mad and making me glad; putting an end to that 'go slow' crap and

*Source: Eldridge Cleaver, *Soul on Ice* (New York: Dell, 1968), pp. 26–27.

putting sweet Watts on the map—my black ass is in Folsom this morning but my black heart is in Watts!" Tears of joy were rolling from his eyes.

It was a cleansing, revolutionary laugh we all shared, something we have not often had occasion for.

Watts was a place of shame. We used to use Watts as an epithet in much the same way as city boys used "country" as a term of derision. To deride one as a "lame," who did not know what was happening (a rustic bumpkin), the "in-crowd" of the time from L.A. would bring a cat down by saying that he had just left Watts, that he ought to go back to Watts until he had learned what was happening, or that he had just stolen enough money to move out of Watts and was already trying to play a cool part. But now, blacks are seen in Folsom saying, "I'm from Watts, Baby!"—whether true or no, but I think their meaning is clear. Confession: I too, have participated in this game, saying, I'm from Watts. In fact, I did live there for a time, and I'm *proud* of it, the tired lamentations of Whitney Young, Roy Wilkins, and The Preacher notwithstanding.

DOCUMENT NO. 15

REPORT OF THE NATIONAL ADVISORY COMMISSION ON CIVIL DISORDERS*

Following the "long hot summer" of 1967 in which major riots broke out in Newark, Detroit, and Cleveland, Johnson appointed the National Advisory Commission on Civil Disorders and charged its members with determining the cause of the riots. The Kerner commission, as it was called because it was headed by Illinois Governor Otto Kerner, was made up of moderates including New York Mayor John Lindsay, Roy Wilkins of the NAACP, and Senator Edward Brooke of Massachusetts. The report of the commission was largely ignored by Johnson. What follows is the introduction and the conclusion of the report.

γ   γ   γ

The summer of 1967 again brought racial disorders to American cities, and with them shock, fear and bewilderment to the nation.

The worst came during a two-week period in July, first in Newark and then in Detroit. Each set off a chain reaction in neighboring communities.

On July 28, 1967, the President of the United States established this Commission and directed us to answer three basic questions:

What happened?
Why did it happen?
What can be done to prevent it from happening again?

To respond to these questions, we have undertaken a broad range of studies and investigations. We have visited the riot cities; we have heard many witnesses; we have sought the counsel of experts across the country.

This is our basic conclusion: Our nation is moving toward two societies, one black, one white—separate and unequal.

Reaction to last summer's disorders has quickened the movement and deepened the division. Discrimination and segregation have long per-

*Source: *Report of the National Advisory Commission on Civil Disorders* (Washington D.C., U.S. Government Printing Office, 1968).

meated much of American life; they now threaten the future of every American.

This deepening racial division is not inevitable. The movement apart can be reversed. Choice is still possible. Our principal task is to define that choice and to press for a national resolution.

To pursue our present course will involve the continuing polarization of the American community and, ultimately, the destruction of basic democratic values.

The alternative is not blind repression or capitulation to lawlessness. It is the realization of common opportunities for all within a single society.

This alternative will require a commitment to national action—compassionate, massive and sustained, backed by the resources of the most powerful and the richest nation on this earth. From every American it will require new attitudes, new understanding, and, above all, new will.

The vital needs of the nation must be met; hard choices must be made, and, if necessary, new taxes enacted.

Violence cannot build a better society. Disruption and disorder nourish repression, not justice. They strike at the freedom of every citizen. The community cannot—it will not—tolerate coercion and mob rule.

Violence and destruction must be ended—in the streets of the ghetto and in the lives of people.

Segregation and poverty have created in the racial ghetto a destructive environment totally unknown to most white Americans.

What white Americans have never fully understood—but what the Negro can never forget—is that white society is deeply implicated in the ghetto. White institutions created it, white institutions maintain it, and white society condones it.

It is time now to turn with all the purpose at our command to the major unfinished business of this nation. It is time to adopt strategies for action that will produce quick and visible progress. It is time to make good the promises of American democracy to all citizens—urban and rural, white and black, Spanish-surname, American Indian, and every minority group.

Our recommendations embrace three basic principles:

To mount programs on a scale equal to the dimension of the problems:

To aim these programs for high impact in the immediate future in order to close the gap between promise and performance;

To undertake new initiatives and experiments that can change the system of failure and frustration that now dominates the ghetto and weakens our society.

These programs will require unprecedented levels of funding and performance, but they neither probe deeper nor demand more than the problems which called them forth. There can be no higher priority for national action and no higher claim on the nation's conscience. . . .

In the summer of 1967, we have seen in our cities a chain reaction of racial violence. If we are heedless, none of us shall escape the consequences.

The future of our cities is neither something which will just happen nor something which will be imposed upon us by an inevitable destiny. That future will be shaped to an important degree by choices we make now.

We have attempted to set forth the major choices because we believe it is vital for Americans to understand the consequences of our present failure to choose—and then to have to choose wisely.

Three critical conclusions emerge from this analysis:

1. The nation is rapidly moving toward two increasingly separate Americas.

Within two decades, this division could be so deep that it would be almost impossible to unite:

a white society principally located in suburbs, in smaller central cities, and in the peripheral parts of large central cities; and

a Negro society largely concentrated within large central cities. . . .

The Negro society will be permanently relegated to its current status, possibly even if we expend great amounts of money and effort in trying to "gild" the ghetto.

2. In the long run, continuation and expansion of such a permanent division threatens us with two perils.

The first is the danger of sustained violence in our cities. The timing, scale, nature, and repercussions of such violence cannot be foreseen. But if it occurred, it would further destroy our ability to achieve the basic American promises of liberty, justice, and equality.

The second is the danger of a conclusive repudiation of the traditional American ideals of individual dignity, freedom, and equality of opportunity. We will not be able to espouse these ideals meaningfully to the rest of the world, to ourselves, to our children. They may still recite the Pledge of Allegiance and say "one nation . . . indivisible." But they will be learning cynicism, not patriotism.

3. We cannot escape responsibility for choosing the future of our metropolitan areas and the human relations which develop within them. It is a responsibility so critical that even an unconscious choice to continue present policies has the gravest implications.

That we have delayed in choosing or, by delaying, may be making the wrong choice, does not sentence us either to separatism or despair. But we must choose. We will choose. Indeed, we are now choosing.

DOCUMENT NO. 16

WHAT WE WANT, WHAT WE BELIEVE
BLACK PANTHERS, 1966*

The Black Panther party was formed in Oakland, California in 1966, and continues to represent the most radical elements of the civil rights movement. Fiercely nationalist, the Black Panthers considered themselves the defenders of the inhabitants of the black ghetto. What follows is their creed.

γ γ γ

1. WE WANT FREEDOM. **We want power to determine the destiny of our Black Community.**

We believe that black people will not be free until we are able to determine our destiny.

2. **We want full employment for our people.**

We believe that the federal government is responsible and obligated to give every man employment or a guaranteed income. We believe that if the white American businessman will not give full employment, then the means of production should be taken from the businessmen and placed in the community so that the people of the community can organize and employ all of its people and give a high standard of living.

3. **We want an end to the robbery by the white man of our Black Community.**

We believe that this racist government has robbed us and now we are demanding the overdue debt of forty acres and two mules. Forty acres and two mules was promised 100 years ago as restitution for slave labor and mass murder of black people. We will accept the payment in currency which will be distributed to our many communities. The Germans are now aiding the Jews in Israel for the genocide of the Jewish people. The Germans murdered six million Jews. The American racist has taken part in the slaughter of over fifty million black people; therefore, we feel that this is a modest demand that we make.

4. **We want decent housing, fit for shelter of human beings.**

We believe that if the white landlords will not give decent housing to our black community, then the housing and the land should be made

*Source: "Platform and Program of the Black Panther Party"

into cooperatives so that our community, with government aid, can build and make decent housing for its people.

5. We want education for our people that exposes the true nature of this decadent American society. We want education that teaches us our true history and our role in the present-day society.

We believe in an educational system that will give to our people a knowledge of self. If a man does not have knowledge of himself and his position in society and the world, then he has little chance to relate to anything else.

6. We want all black men to be exempt from military service.

We believe that black people should not be forced to fight in the military service to defend a racist government that does not protect us. We will not fight and kill other people of color in the world who, like black people, are being victimized by the white racist government of America. We will protect ourselves from the force and violence of the racist police and the racist military, by whatever means necessary.

7. We want an immediate end to POLICE BRUTALITY and MURDER of black people.

We believe we can end police brutality in our black community by organizing black self-defense groups that are dedicated to defending our black community from racist police oppression and brutality. The Second Amendment to the Constitution of the United States gives a right to bear arms. We therefore believe that all black people should arm themselves for self-defense.

8. We want freedom for all black men held in federal, state, county, and city prisons and jails.

We believe that all black people should be released from the many jails and prisons because they have not received a fair and impartial trial.

9. We want all black people when brought to trial to be tried in court by a jury of their peer group or people from their black communities, as defined by the Constitution of the United States.

We believe that the courts could follow the United States Constitution so that black people will receive fair trials. The 14th Amendment of the U.S. Constitution gives a man a right to be tried by his peer group. A peer is a person from a similar economic, social, religious, geographical, environmental, historical and racial background. To do this the court will be forced to select a jury from the black community from which the black defendant came. We have been, and are being tried by all-white juries that have no understanding of the "average reasoning man" of the black community.

10. We want land, bread, housing, education, clothing, justice and peace. And as our major political objective, a United Nations-supervised plebiscite to be held throughout the black colony in which only black colonial subjects will be allowed to participate, for the purpose of determining the will of black people as to their national destiny.

When, in the course of human events, it becomes necessary for one people to dissolve the political bands which have connected them with another, and to assume, among the powers of the earth, the separate and equal station to which the laws of nature and nature's God entitle them, a decent respect to the opinions of mankind requires that they should declare the causes which impel them to the separation.

We hold these truths to be self-evident, that all men are created equal; that they are endowed by their Creator with certain unalienable rights; that among these are life, liberty, and the pursuit of happiness. That, to secure these rights, governments are instituted among men, deriving their just powers from the consent of the governed; that, whenever any form of government becomes destructive of these ends, it is the right of the people to alter or to abolish it, and to institute a new government, laying its foundation on such principles, and organizing its powers in such form, as to them shall seem most likely to effect their safety and happiness. Prudence, indeed, will dictate that governments long established should not be changed for light and transient causes; and, accordingly, all experience hath shown, that mankind are more disposed to suffer, while evils are sufferable, than to right themselves by abolishing the forms to which they are accustomed. But, when a long train of abuses and usurpations, pursuing invariably the same object, evinces a design to reduce them under absolute despotism, it is their right, it is their duty, to throw off such government, and to provide new guards for their future security.

DOCUMENT NO. 17

AFFIRMATIVE ACTION AND
THE BAKKE DECISION*

In the late 1960s the federal government went beyond leading the nation in ending racial segregation and discrimination in education, housing, and employment and began promoting a policy of "affirmative action" through programs aimed at increasing opportunities in education and employment for African Americans, women, and other minority groups. These affirmative action programs ranged from aggressive recruiting of minorities, to set-asides and quotas designed to award an exact number of jobs, or percentage of admissions, to blacks, women and other minorities. By the 1970s, the Department of Health, Education and Welfare had issued guidelines and threatened to withhold federal funds from colleges and universities that failed to meet hiring and admissions goals for blacks, women, and other minorities.

However, in 1978 the Supreme Court held in Regents of the University of California v. Bakke *that fixed admissions quotas for racial minorities at the University of California at Davis medical school were unconstitutional. The court decision was split, but a majority of the justices rejected the use of racial quotas as a means of overcoming accumulated handicaps that past acts of racism had imposed on blacks and other minority groups. The impact of the case reinforced a growing white opposition to what was being called "reverse discrimination" and weakened the commitment of private and public agencies to aid blacks and other minority groups in achieving equality by considering race in their hiring and admissions policies.*

What follows is a portion of Justice Lewis F. Powell's decision of the court. Powell's opinion does not strike down affirmative action programs, but he declares unconstitutional quota systems of the type in use at U.C.-Davis. Bakke was admitted.

γ γ γ

It may be assumed that the reservation of a specified number of seats in each class for individuals from the preferred ethnic groups would contribute to the attainment of considerable ethnic diversity in the student body. But petitioner's argument that this is the only effective

*Source: 438 U.S. 265, 98 S. Ct. 2733 (1978)

means of serving the interest of diversity is seriously flawed. In a most fundamental sense the argument misconceives the nature of the state interest that would justify consideration of race or ethnic background. It is not an interest in simple ethnic diversity, in which a specified percentage of the student body is in effect guaranteed to be members of selected ethnic groups, with the remaining percentage an undifferentiated aggregation of students. The diversity that furthers a compelling state interest encompasses a far broader array of qualifications and characteristics of which racial or ethnic origin is but a single though important element. Petitioner's special admissions program, focused *solely* on ethnic diversity, would hinder rather than further attainment of genuine diversity. . . .

In summary, it is evident that the Davis special admissions program involves the use of an explicit racial classification never before countenanced by this Court. It tells applicants who are not Negro, Asian, or Chicano that they are totally excluded from a specific percentage of the seats in an entering class. No matter how strong their qualifications, quantitative and extracurricular, including their own potential for contribution to educational diversity, they are never afforded the chance to compete with applicants from the preferred groups for the special admissions seats. At the same time, the preferred applicants have the opportunity to compete for every seat in the class.

The fatal flaw in petitioner's preferential program is its disregard of individual rights as guaranteed by the Fourteenth Amendment. Such rights are not absolute. But when a State's distribution of benefits or imposition of burdens hinges on ancestry or the color of a person's skin, that individual is entitled to a demonstration that the challenged classification is necessary to promote a substantial state interest. Petitioner has failed to carry this burden. For this reason, that portion of the California court's judgment holding petitioner's special admissions program invalid under the Fourteenth Amendment must be affirmed.

In enjoining petitioner from ever considering the race of any applicant, however, the courts below failed to recognize that the State has a substantial interest that legitimately may be served by a properly devised admissions program involving the competitive consideration of race and ethnic origin. For this reason, so much of the California court's judgment as enjoins petitioner from any consideration of the race of any applicant must be reversed.

DOCUMENT NO. 18

JESSE JACKSON AND THE
POSTREFORM CIVIL RIGHTS MOVEMENT*

Following Martin Luther King's assassination in April 1968 the leadership of the nonviolent protest movement fell by default to a young protege of King's, Jesse Jackson. In 1971 Jackson formed Operation PUSH (People United to Save Humanity); and by the early 1980s he had become the most visible civil rights activist in the nation. Jackson made two unsuccessful bids for the Democratic party nomination in 1984 and 1988. In the following address, delivered at the 1988 Democratic party convention in Atlanta, Jackson recalls the leaders of the civil rights reform period.

γ   γ   γ

Tonight we pause and give praise and honor to God for being good enough to allow us to be at this place at this time. . . . We're really standing on someone's shoulders. Ladies and gentlemen. Mrs. Rosa Parks. . . .

Twenty-four years ago, the late Fannie Lou Hamer and Aaron Henry—who sits here tonight from Mississippi—were locked out on the streets of Atlantic City, the head of the Mississippi Freedom Democratic Party. But tonight, a black and white delegation from Mississippi is headed by Ed Cole, a black man, from Mississippi.

. . . Many were lost in the struggle for the right to vote. Jimmy Lee Jackson, a young student, gave his life. Viola Liuzzo, a white mother from Detroit, called nigger lover, had her brains blown out at point blank range. Schwerner, Goodman and Chaney—two Jews and a black—found in a common grave, bodies riddled with bullets in Mississippi. The four little girls in the church in Birmingham, Alabama. They died that we might have a right to live.

Dr. Martin Luther King, Jr. lies only a few miles from us tonight. Tonight he must feel good as he looks down upon us. We sit here together, a rainbow, a coalition—the sons and daughters of slave masters and the sons and daughters of slaves sitting together around a common table, to decide the direction of our party and our country. His heart would be full tonight.

*Source: *Vital Speeches* LIV, pp. 649–653.

As a testament to the struggles of those who have gone before; as a legacy for those who will come after . . . their work has not been in vain, and hope is eternal; tomorrow night my name will go into nomination for the presidency of the United States of America.

We meet tonight at a crossroads, a point of decision. Shall we expand, be inclusive, find unity and power; or suffer division and impotence.

We come to Atlanta, the cradle of the old south, the crucible of the new South. Tonight there is a sense of celebration because we are moved, fundamentally moved, from racial battlegrounds by law, to economic common ground, tomorrow we will challenge to move to higher ground.

Common ground! . . .

Many people, many cultures, many languages—with one thing in common, the yearning to be free.

Common ground! . . .

The good of our nation is at stake—its commitment to working men and women, to the poor and vulnerable, to the many in the world. With so many guided missiles, and so much misguided leadership, the stakes are exceedingly high. Our choice, full participation in a Democratic government, or more abandonment and neglect. And so this night, we choose not a false sense of independence, not our capacity to act and unite for the greater good. The common good is finding commitment to new priorities, to expansion and inclusion. A commitment to expanded participation in the Democratic Party at every level. . . .

Common ground. Easier said than done. Where do you find common ground at the point of challenge? . . .

We find common ground at the plant gate that closes on workers without notice. We find common ground at the farm auction where a good farmer loses his or her land to bad loans or diminishing markets. Common ground at the schoolyard where teachers cannot get adequate pay, and students cannot get a scholarship and can't make a loan. Common ground at the hospital admitting room where somebody tonight is dying because they cannot afford to go upstairs to a bed that's empty, waiting for someone with insurance to get sick. We are a better nation than that. We must do better. . . .

America's not a blanket woven from one thread, one color, one cloth. When I was a child growing up in Greenville, S.C., and grandmother could not afford a blanket, she didn't complain and we did not freeze. Instead, she took pieces of old cloth—patches, wool, silk, gabardine, crockersak on the patches—barely good enough to wipe off your shoes with.

But they didn't stay that way very long. With sturdy hands and a strong cord, she sewed them together into a quilt, a thing of beauty and power and culture. Now, Democrats, we must build such a quilt. . . .

But don't despair. Be as wise as my grandma. Pool the patches and the pieces together, bound by a common thread. When we form a great quilt of unity and common ground we'll have the power to bring about health care and housing and jobs and education and hope to our nation.

We the people can win. We stand at the end of a long dark night of reaction. We stand tonight united in a commitment to a new direction. For almost eight years, we've been led by those who view social good coming from private interest, who view public life as a means to increase private wealth. They have been prepared to sacrifice the common good of the many to satisfy the private interest and the wealth of a few. We believe in a government that's a tool of our democracy in service to the public, not an instrument of the aristocracy. . . .

Wherever you are tonight, I challenge you to hope and to dream. Don't submerge your dreams . . . dream of things as they ought to be. Dream. Face pain, but love, hope, faith, and dreams will help you rise above the pain. . . . Don't surrender and don't give up.

When I was born late one afternoon, October 8th, in Greenville, S.C., no writers asked my mother her name. Nobody chose to write down our address. My mama was not supposed to make it. And I was not supposed to make it. You see, I was born to a teen-age mother who was born to a teen-age mother.

I understand. I know abandonment. . . . I wasn't born in the hospital. . . . I was not born with a silver spoon in my mouth. I had a shovel programmed for my hand. My mother, a working woman. . . . I was born in the slum, but the slum was not born in me. And it wasn't born in you, and you can make it. . . .

You must not surrender. You may or may not get there, but just know that you're qualified and you hold on and hold out. We must never surrender. America will get better and better. Keep hope alive. . . . On tomorrow night and beyond, keep hope alive. . . .

DOCUMENT NO. 19

LOUIS FARRAKHAN CALLS FOR A HOLY DAY OF ATONEMENT AND RECONCILIATION OCTOBER 16, 1995*

The Nation of Islam had, through the 1980s and early 1990s, occupied the most radical reaches of the civil rights movement. Under the leadership of Louis Farrakhan, the NOI espoused racial separatism, virulent anti-Semitism, and hatred. This radical stance, represented most visibly in several speeches by NOI representative Khalid Muhammad, further split the races, which it in turn fed the white backlash. By the mid-1990s black-on-black crime, drug abuse in black neighborhoods, rising black unemployment, the South Central riots, and the racial connotations of the O.J. Trial had driven the nation into a racial turmoil that approached the magnitude of the late-1960s.

By calling for a Holy Day of Atonement and Reconciliation, Louis Farrakhan clearly hoped to heal some of the wounds inside the black community while putting a more moderate face on the NOI. In the press release excerpted below Farrakhan recounts the problems in America's black communities. He then calls all African American males to the Holy Day in Washington, D.C., October 16, 1995. The event would become the Million Man March.

γ   γ   γ

. . . We, in leadership, must do all within our power to get out of this prophesied woe. Therefore, we are calling on the religious leaders in the Black community to assert our freedom by declaring our first Holy Day, A Holy Day of Atonement and Reconciliation. The religious leaders must lead the way in atonement.

Many of our people ask the question, "Atone for what and to whom?" First, it is Allah (God) who is calling us to come out of the mentality of a slave into the vast world of freedom of thought and action on behalf of self, family, and nation. Our failure to accept the call of Allah (God) to be the responsible heads of our families and community is our principle failure. Therefore, we as a people must atone to Allah (God) for our failure to accept the call to freedom. We, as men, must atone for the

*Source: Cable News Network

abuse of our women and girls, and our failure to be the leaders of and builders of our community.

We must atone for the destruction that is going on within our communities; the fratricide, the death dealing drugs, and the violence that plagues us. Our atonement is first to Allah (God) that He may return to us power and dominion to take control of our lives, destiny, and our community.

We must then reconcile our differences one with the other so that we may face our oppressors as a solid wall of unity. We have spent valuable time petitioning government and to a degree government heard us but now government is reversing the gains that our suffering and petition has brought about. We petitioned the wrong source. Our petition must now be to the Author of all creation. For, if we satisfy His requirements, then, He shall return to us the power bound up in His Spirit and Word and the dominion that comes from the proper use of His Wisdom, then, we would not need to beg any man for what Allah (God) has Divinely Ordered as the right of every human being. We will have the power to give these rights to ourselves.

Atone. To whom and for what? II Chronicles, Chapter 7:14 reads, "If my people, which are called by my name, shall humble themselves, and pray, and seek my face, and turn from their wicked ways; then will I hear from heaven, and will forgive their sin, and will heal their land." The above mentioned scripture is the key to our deliverance, but, we cannot get Allah's (God's) healing until we fulfill the precondition. Therefore, Monday, October 16th, a work day, we are asking a million Black men to descend on Washington to present our bodies as a reasonable sacrifice.

In the Book of Romans, Chapter 12, verses 1-2 it reads, "I BESEECH you therefore, brethren, by the mercies of God, that ye present your bodies a living sacrifice, holy, acceptable to God, which is your reasonable service. And be not conformed to this world: but be ye transformed by the renewing of your mind, that ye may prove what is that good, and acceptable, and perfect, will of God."

Our presence in Washington in unity is an act of atonement. Our prayers together is what is required. If we are able to fast from sun up till sun down, that is a requirement, then, we as a people must make up our minds to turn away from that which Allah (God) declares is wicked. If we do this, like the prodigal son, we will have made a step toward the

Father and He will make two toward us, then, He will hear from heaven, forgive our sins, and heal our land.

According to the International Standard Bible Encyclopedia atonement means, "To cover, expiate, condone, cancel, placate; to offer or receive a sin offering, appease, propitiate; effect reconciliation by some conduct, or course of action; to cause to be friendly; to render other, hence to restore; to leave off, i.e. enmity or evil; to render holy, to set apart for; hence of the Deity, to appropriate or accept for Himself." We have to be at-one with Allah (God). We have to be at peace with Allah (God) and then we must make a concerted effort to be at peace with each other.

We are asking all those who have differences in their family to seek reconciliation. Those of us who have variances within our churches, mosques, synagogues or temples should seek reconciliation. Those of us involved in the struggle who have knowingly and unknowingly offended each other must reconcile our differences. All the religious houses in the Black community should be open so that those who have differences within those religious houses may come and reconcile their differences and pray for the success and well being of those in Washington and for Allah (God) to send His Spirit upon us and to heal our communities.

Let the bells on religious houses toll. Sound the ram horn and let the Muezzin at the mosques sound the call to prayer.

Those who are not able to make it, the men and the women, can support the March and Day of Atonement by our act of reasonable sacrifice. We should declare this Holy Day, A Day of Absence, from a racist system that refuses to recognize our contributions to this nation and to give us justice.

We all should register our dissatisfaction with the way that we are being treated. We should not go to work or school; none of us should participate in any shopping, sport or play; none of us should drink any alcohol or use any drugs or do any unclean thing during this Holy Day. We are asking the mothers to be with their children teaching them the value of home, self, family, and unity, reconciling differences within the family.

We are also asking the nearly eight million Black persons who are eligible to vote, but are unregistered, to go to their house of worship on that day, October 16th to register.

The most fateful election of this century will be held in 1996. We will, if properly instructed, hold the balance of power. No political party ever again will take our vote for granted.

America must be made to know her sins that she may, if she will, atone for her evils done to Black people, the Native Americans, and others. Whether America atones or not, we must draw our strength from Allah (God) through the fulfillment of the precondition laid down in the scriptures.

When you read this article take it and discuss it with others. Let us show the world that we are ready to receive the goodly substance that Allah (God) promised us after our sojourn, affliction, suffering, and death for 400 years in this modern land of bondage.

Will you join me in Washington and/or in the observance of this Holy Day of Atonement and Reconciliation.

May Allah (God) bless us to be in that number when the Saints go marching in.

DOCUMENT NO. 20

BILL CLINTON ATTEMPTS TO
HEAL THE NATION'S WOUNDS
OCTOBER 16, 1995*

Bill Clinton's campaign strategy that led to his election in 1992 largely spurned black votes in hopes of carrying the South and tapping into some of the Northern white backlash votes that had carried Ronald Reagan and George Bush into the White House through the 1980s. By the mid-1990s, however, racial tensions in the nation had reached fever pitch, higher than at any point since the end of the 1960s. The national mood demanded a response from the White House, and Bill Clinton responded by delivering his first, last, and only major speech on civil rights. Clinton's speech, excerpted below, was clearly heartfelt and honest, but it did not fit his political philosophy, and it probably did not help the Democratic party in the 1996 interim elections.

The speech was delivered at the University of Texas on October 16, 1995, the day of the Million Man March in Washington and just two weeks after the O. J. Simpson verdict was handed down.

γ   γ   γ

. . . In recent weeks everyone of us has been made aware of a simple truth. White Americans and black Americans often see the same world in drastically different ways. Ways that go beyond and beneath the Simpson trial and its aftermath, which brought these perceptions so starkly into the open.

The rift we see before us that is tearing at the heart of America exists in spite of the remarkable progress black Americans have made in the last generation since Martin Luther King swept America up in his dream and President Johnson spoke so powerfully for the dignity of man and the destiny of democracy in demanding that Congress guarantee full voting rights to blacks.

The rift between blacks and whites exists still in a very special way in America, in spite of the fact that we have become much more racially and ethnically diverse. And that, Hispanic Americans, themselves no

*Source: White House press release

strangers to discrimination, are now almost ten percent of our national population.

The reasons for this divide are many. Some are rooted in the awful history and stubborn persistence of racism. Some are rooted in the different ways we experience the threats of modern life to personal security, family values and strong communities.

Some are rooted in the fact that we still haven't learned to talk frankly, to listen carefully, and to work together across racial lines.

Almost 30 years ago, Dr. Martin Luther King took his last march with sanitation workers in Memphis. They marched for dignity, equality and economic justice. Many carried placards that read simply, "I am a man." The throngs of men marching in Washington today, almost all of them are doing so for the same stated reason, but there is a profound difference between this march today, and those of 30 years ago.

Thirty years ago, the marchers were demanding the dignity and opportunity they were due because in the face of terrible discrimination they had worked hard, raised their children, paid their taxes, obeyed the laws and fought our wars.

Well, today's march is also about pride and dignity and respect. But after a generation of deepening social problems that disproportionately impact black Americans, it is also about black men taking renewed responsibility for themselves, their families and their communities.

It's about saying "no" to crime and drugs and violence. It's about standing up for atonement and reconciliation. It's about insisting that others do the same and offering to help them. It's about the frank admission that, unless black men shoulder their load, no one else can help them or their brothers, their sisters and their children escape the hard, bleak lives that too many of them still face.

Of course, some of those in the March do have a history that is far from its message of atonement and reconciliation. One million men are right to be standing up for personal responsibility. But one million men do not make right one man's message of malice and division.

No good house was ever built on a bad foundation. Nothing good ever came of hate. So let us pray today that all who march and all who speak will stand for atonement, for reconciliation, for responsibility.

Let us pray that those who have spoken for hatred and division in the past will turn away from that past and give voice to the true message of those ordinary Americans who march. If that happens . . .

If that happens, the men and the women who are there with them will be marching into better lives for themselves and their families and they could be marching into a better future for America.

Today, we face a choice. One way leads to further separation and bitterness and more lost futures. The other way—the path of courage and wisdom—leads to unity, to reconciliation, to a rich opportunity for all Americans to make the most of the lives God gave them.

This moment, in which the racial divide is so clearly out in the open need not be a setback for us. It presents us with a great opportunity and we dare not let it pass us by.

In the past, when we've had the courage to face the truth about our failure to live up to our own best ideals, we've grown stronger, moved forward, and restored proud American optimism. At such turning points, America moved to preserve the Union and abolish slavery, to embrace women's suffrage, to guarantee basic legal rights to America without regard to race under the leadership of President Johnson.

At each of these moments, we looked in the national mirror, and were brave enough to say, this is not who we are. We're better than that.

Abraham Lincoln reminded us that "a house divided against itself, can not stand." When divisions have threatened to bring our house down, somehow we have always moved together to shore it up.

My fellow Americans, our house is the greatest democracy in all human history. And with all its racial and ethnic diversity it has beaten the odds of human history. But we know that divisions remain. And we still have work to do.

The two worlds we see now, each can't contain both truth and distortion. Both black and white Americans must face this, for honesty is the only gateway to the many acts of reconciliations that will unite our worlds at last into one America.

White America must understand and acknowledge the roots of black pain. It began with unequal treatment, first in law, and later in fact. African Americans, indeed, have lived too long with a justice system that in too many cases has been and continues to be, less than just.

The record of abuses extends from lynchings and trumped up charges to false arrests and police brutality. The tragedies of Emmett Till and Rodney King are bloody markers on the very same road. Still today too many of our police officers play by the rules of the bad old days. It is beyond wrong when law abiding black parents have to tell their law abiding children to fear the police whose salaries are paid by their own taxes.

And blacks are right to think something is terribly wrong when African American men are many times more likely to be victims of homicide than any other group in this country; when there are more African American men in our correction system than in our colleges; when almost one in three African American men, in their twenties, are either in jail, on parole, or otherwise under the supervision of the criminal system. Nearly one in three.

And that is a disproportionate percentage in comparison to the percent of blacks who use drugs in our society. Now I would like every white person here and in America to take a moment to think how he or she would feel if one in three white men were in similar circumstances.

And there is still unacceptable economic disparity between blacks and whites. It is so fashionable to talk, today, about African Americans, as if they had been some sort of protected class. Many whites think blacks are getting more than their fair share, in terms of jobs and promotions. That is not true. That is not true.

The truth is that African Americans still make on average about 60 percent of what white people do. And more than half of African American children live in poverty and at the very time our young Americans need access to college more than ever before, black college enrollment is dropping in America.

On the other hand, blacks must understand and acknowledge the roots of white fear in America.

There is a legitimate fear of the violence that is too prevalent in our urban areas and often, by experience or at least what people see on the news at night, violence for those white people too often has a black face.

It isn't racist for a parent to pull his or her child close when walking through a high crime neighborhood. Or, to wish to stay away from neighborhoods where innocent children can be shot in school or standing at bus stops by thugs driving by with assault weapons or toting handguns like old west desperadoes.

It isn't racist for parents to recoil in disgust when they read about a national survey of gang members saying that two thirds of them feel justified in shooting someone simply for showing them disrespect.

It isn't racist for whites to say they don't understand why people put up with gangs on the corner or in the projects or with drugs being sold in the schools or in the open. It's not racist for whites to assert that the culture of welfare dependency, out of wedlock pregnancy and absent fatherhood cannot be broken by social programs, unless there is first more personal responsibility.

The great potential for this march today, beyond the black community, is that whites will come to see a larger truth. That blacks share their fears and embrace their convictions; openly assert that, without changes in the black community and within individuals, real change for our society will not come.

This march could remind white people that most black people share their old fashioned American values.

For most black Americans still do work hard, care for their families, pay their taxes and obey the law. Often, under circumstances which are far more difficult than those their white counterparts face.

Imagine how you would feel if you were a young parent in your twenties with a young child living in a housing project, working somewhere for $5 an hour with no health insurance, passing every day, people on the street selling drugs, making one hundred times what you make. Those people are the real heroes of America today and we should recognize that.

And white people too often forget that they are not immune to the problems black Americans face. Crime, drugs, domestic abuse and teen pregnancy. They are too prevalent among whites as well and some of those problems are growing faster in our white population than in our minority population.

So, we all have a stake in solving these common problems together. It is, therefore, wrong for white Americans to do what they have done too often, simply to move further away from the problems and support policies that will only make them worse.

Finally, both sides seem to fear deep down inside that they'll never quite be able to see each other as more than enemy faces, all of whom carry at least a sliver of bigotry in their hearts.

Differences of opinion rooted in different experiences are healthy, indeed essential for democracies. But differences so great and so rooted in race, threaten to divide the house Mr. Lincoln gave his life to save. As Dr. King said, we must learn to live together as brothers, or we will perish as fools.

Recognizing one another's real grievances is only the first step. We must all take responsibility for ourselves, our conduct and our attitudes.

America we must clean our house of racism. . . . White racism may be black people's burden, but it's white people's problem. We must clean our house.

To our black citizens, I honor the presence of hundreds of thousands of men in Washington today, committed to atonement and to personal responsibility. And the commitment of millions of other men and women who are African Americans to this cause. I call upon you to build on this effort, to share equally in the promise of America. But to do that, your house too must be cleaned of racism. . . .

BIBLIOGRAPHY

The best place to begin is with general surveys of the civil rights movement. The series being compiled by Taylor Branch is quickly becoming the most important history of the movement. His first volume, *Parting the Waters: America in the King Years* (New York: Simon and Schuster, 1989), covers the period from 1954 to 1963. His second volume, *Pillar of Fire: America in the King Years* (New York: Simon and Schuster, 1998), takes an in-depth look at the two-year period between 1963 and 1965. Two less ambitious, but certainly useful accounts include Harvard Sitkoff, *The Struggle for Black Equality, 1954–1980* (New York: Hill and Wang, 1992); and Steven F. Lawson, *Running for Freedom: Civil Rights and Black Politics in America since 1941* (New York, McGraw-Hill, 1991). Lawson carries the movement up into the late 1980s. Other surveys include Robert Weisbrot, *Freedom Bound: A History of America's Civil Rights Movement* (New York: Dutton, 1991); and Juan Williams's companion to the PBS series, *Eyes on the Prize: America's Civil Rights Years, 1954–1965* (New York: Viking-Penguin, 1987). The photographs and interviews here are useful. Manning Marable looks at civil rights from a viewpoint that the movement was too conservative in his *Race, Reform, and Rebellion: The Second Reconstruction in Black America* (Jackson, Mississippi, University of Mississippi, 1991). See also Marable's *Black Leadership* (New York: Columbia University, 1998). Intelligently constructed conservative treatments of the movement include Thomas Sowell, *Civil Rights: Rhetoric or Reality?* (New York: William Morrow, 1985); and James J. Kilpatrick, *The Southern Case of School Segregation* (New York: Crowell-Collier, 1962).

There are some excellent documentary histories available. See particularly David J. Garrow's three volumes, *We Shall Overcome: The Civil Rights Movement in the United States in the 1950s and 1960s* (New York: Carlson, 1989); and Garrow et. al., *Eyes on the Prize Civil Rights Reader: Documents, Speeches and Firsthand Accounts for the Black Freedom Movement, 1954–1990* (New York: Viking-Penguin, 1991). See also Peter B. Levy, *Let Freedom Ring: A Documentary History of the Civil Rights Movement* (Westport, Connecticut: Praeger, 1992); and Albert P. Blaustein and Robert L. Zangrando, *Civil Rights and the American Negro; A Documentary History* (Chicago: Northwestern University, 1992). A compilation of King's writings is James M. Washington, *A Testament*

143

of Hope; The Essential Speeches and Writings of Martin Luther King, Jr. (San Francisco: Harper, 1990). A good oral history of the movement can be found in Howell Raines, *My Soul Is Rested: Movement Days in the Deep South Remembered* (New York: Viking Penguin, 1983). This is an excellent balance of interviews with both leaders and soldiers.

On the era preceding the modern civil rights movement in the South, C. Vann Woodward's *The Strange Career of Jim Crow* (Baton Rouge: Louisiana State University, 3rd ed., 1990) still stands the test of time, particularly in its discussion of the legal battles prior to the *Brown* decision. This third edition carries Woodward's story up to about 1970. A work that looks at the origins of the movement at the grassroots level is Aldon D. Morris, *The Origins of the Civil Rights Movement: Black Communities Organize for Change* (New York: Free Press, 1986). Also on black issues and concerns in the decades before the modern movement is John Egerton, *Speak Now Against the Day: The Generation Before the Civil Rights Movement in the South* (Chapel Hill: University of North Carolina, 1995). Nancy Weiss looks at why blacks became Democrats in *Farewell to the Party of Lincoln: Black Politics in the Age of FDR* (Princeton, New Jersey: Princeton University, 1983). See also Harvard Sitkoff, *A New Deal for Blacks* (New York: Oxford University, 1978). On A. Philip Randolph and the 1941 March on Washington Movement, see Herbert Garfinkel, *When Negroes March* (New York: Simon and Schuster, 1985). The best biography of Randolph is Paula F. Pfeffer, *A. Philip Randolph: Pioneer of the Civil Rights Movement* (Baton Rouge: Louisiana State University, 1990). There are several excellent biographies of Martin Luther King. The best place to start is Dave J. Garrow's Pulitzer Prize winning, *Bearing the Cross: Martin Luther King, Jr., and the Southern Christian Leadership Conference* (New York: William Morrow, 1986); and Stephen B. Oates, *Let the Trumpet Sound: The Life of Martin Luther King, Jr.* (New York: Harper, 1982). Both are excellent works. Other biographies include James A. Colaiaco, *Martin Luther King, Jr.: Apostle of Militant Nonviolence* (New York: St. Martin, 1993); David Levering Lewis, *King: A Biography* (Urbana: University of Illinois, 1978); and Adam Fairclough, *To Redeem the Soul of America: The Southern Christian Leadership Conference and Martin Luther King, Jr.* (Athens: University of Georgia, 1987). A collection of King's writings, mentioned above, is James M. Washington, *A Testament of Hope*.

King left four books on the movement. All are useful. His own account of the Montgomery bus boycott is *Stride Toward Freedom: The*

Montgomery Story (New York: Harper and Brothers, 1958). His plea for federal civil rights legislation is *Why We Can't Wait* (New York: New American Library, 1964). See also *The Trumpet of Conscience* (New York: Harper and Row, 1968). And finally, his analysis of the movement's divisions in the mid-1960s is, *Where Do We Go from Here? Chaos or Community?* (New York: Harper and Row, 1967).

There are several important histories and memoirs written by the movement's participants. See particularly John Lewis, *Walking With the Wind: A Memoir of the Movement* (New York: Simon and Schuster, 1998); Andrew Young, *An Easy Burden: The Civil Rights Movement and the Transformation of America* (New York: Harper Collins, 1996); Ralph Abernathy, *And the Walls Came Tumbling Down* (New York: Harper Collins, 1989); James Farmer, *Lay Bare the Heart: An Autobiography of the Civil Rights Movement* (New York: Arbor House, 1985); Bayard Rustin's recollections and observations, *Down the Line* (Chicago: Quadrangle, 1971); and *Strategies for Freedom: The Changing Patterns of Black Protest* (New York: Columbia, 1976). See also Coretta Scott King's story of the movement, published just after her husband's assassination, *My Life with Martin Luther King, Jr.* (New York: Holt, Rinehart and Winston, 1969). Jo Ann Robinson was an important figure in the Montgomery bus boycott. Her memoir, edited by David J. Garrow, is *The Montgomery Bus Boycott and the Women Who Started It* (Knoxville, University of Tennessee, 1987). In 1967 Stokely Carmichael and Charles V. Hamilton tried almost desperately to define black power in *Black Power: The Politics of Liberation in America* (New York: Random House, 1967). There is probably no greater source for understanding the radical side of the movement than *The Autobiography of Malcolm X* (New York: Grove Press, 1964). Others include Floyd McKissick, *Three-Fifths of A Man* (New York: Macmillan, 1969); and James Farmer, *Freedom—When?* (New York: Random House, 1965).

There are a number of works that explore specific aspects of the movement. On the *Brown* decision, a good place to start is Richard Kruger, *Simple Justice: The History of Brown v. Board of Education and Black America's Struggle for Equality* (New York: Vintage, 1977). On the sit-in movement, the standard work is William Chafe, *Civilities and Civil Rights: Greensboro, North Carolina, and the Black Struggle for Freedom* (New York: Oxford University, 1981). On that same topic, see Martin Oppenheimer, *The Sit-In Movement of 1960* (New York: Carlson, 1989). On the Freedom Summer of 1964, see Doug McAdam, *Freedom*

Summer (New York: Oxford University, 1988). On Selma, see David J. Garrow, *Protest at Selma: Martin Luther King, Jr., and the Voting Rights Act of 1965* (New Haven: Yale University, 1978). An interesting look at the beginnings of the movement is David Halberstam, *The Children* (New York: Random House, 1998). Here Halberstam looks at his own experiences as a journalist in the South as the movement was just getting off the ground in the early sixties. Another important work is Stephen F. Lawson, *Black Ballots: Voting Rights in the South, 1944–1969* (New York: Columbia University, 1976).

There are a number of important works on the various civil rights organizations. On the NAACP, the standard work is Charles Flint Kellogg, *NAACP: A History of the National Association for the Advancement of Colored People* (Baltimore: Johns Hopkins University, 1967). On the SCLC, Adam Fairclough's aforementioned, *To Redeem the Soul of America: The Southern Christian Leadership Conference and Martin Luther King, Jr.* is as much a biography of King as a history of the SCLC. The best work on the SNCC is Clayborne Carson, *In Struggle: SNCC and the Black Awakening of the 1960s* (Boston: Harvard University, 1981). Howard Zinn, a leader in the early days of the SNCC, has written about the organization in his *SNCC: The New Abolitionists* (Boston: Beacon, 1965). On CORE, the best work is August Meier and Elliot Rudwick, *CORE: A Study in the Civil Rights Movement, 1942–1968* (Urbana: University of Illinois, 1973). On the Urban League, see Nancy Weiss's biography of Whitney Young, *Whitney M. Young and the Struggle for Civil Rights* (Princeton, New Jersey: Princeton University, 1989); and Dennis C. Dickerson, *Whitney M. Young, Jr.: Militant Mediator* (Lexington: University of Kentucky, 1998).

The civil rights movement was often defined by the relationship between the movement and the federal government. On this point, see Steven A. Shull, *The President and Civil Rights Policy: Leadership and Change* (Westport, Connecticut: Greenwood, 1990); and Hugh Davis Graham, *The Civil Rights Era: Origins and Development of National Policy, 1960–1972* (New York: Oxford University, 1990). For the Roosevelt administration, see the aforementioned work by Nancy Weiss, *Farewell to the Party of Lincoln*. On the Truman administration, see William C. Berman, *The Politics of Civil Rights in the Truman Administration* (Lexington: University of Kentucky, 1970). On Eisenhower and civil rights, the best works are Robert Frederick Burk, *The Eisenhower Administra-*

tion and Black Civil Rights (Knoxville: University of Tennessee, 1984); and Allan Wolk, *The Presidency and Black Civil Rights: Eisenhower to Nixon* (Teaneck, New Jersey: Fairleigh Dickinson University, 1971). On Kennedy and civil rights, see Carl M. Bauer, *John F. Kennedy and the Second Reconstruction* (New York: Columbia University, 1977); Victor Navasky, *Kennedy Justice* (New York: Scribner, 1977); and Mark Stern, *Calculating Vision: Kennedy, Johnson, and Civil Rights* (Camden, New Jersey: Rutgers University, 1992). Stern's volume works well for Lyndon Johnson and civil rights, but see also James C. Harvey, *Black Civil Rights During the Johnson Administration* (Jackson, Mississippi: University of Mississippi, 1973). On the federal government and civil rights in the 1980s and the 1990s, see Steven A. Shull, *A Kinder, Gentler Racism? The Reagan-Bush Civil Rights Legacy* (Armonk, New York: M. E. Sharpe, 1993). For a broad look at politics in general and the civil rights movement, see Kenneth O'Reilly, *Nixon's Piano: Presidents and Racial Politics from Washington to Clinton* (New York: Free Press, 1995).

Radicalism inside the movement must begin with Malcolm X. His autobiography, published after his death in 1965, had a great impact on the movement. George Breitman has analyzed Malcolm in his *The Last Year of Malcolm X* (New York: Merit, 1967); and in a collection of documents on Malcolm, *By Any Means Necessary: Speeches, Interviews, and a Letter* (New York: Pathfinder, 1970). Both are useful. A good biography is Louis Goldman, *The Death and Life of Malcolm X* (New York: Harper, 1967); it was an important anthem for blacks in the late 1960s and early 1970s.

Newman V. Bartley wrote the first important work on the backlash, focusing specifically on the South and its resistance to civil rights. See his *Rise of Massive Resistance: Race and Politics in the South During the 1950s and 1960s* (Baton Rouge: Louisiana State University, 1969). Dan T. Carter has done some important work here. See his biography of George Wallace, *The Politics of Rage: George Wallace, the Origins of the New Conservatism, and the Transformation of American Politics* (Baton Rouge: Louisiana State University, 1996). Many of Carter's ideas are spelled out more succinctly in his *From George Wallace to Newt Gingrich: Race in the Conservative Counterrevolution, 1963–1994* (Baton Rouge: Louisiana State University, 1996). A sympathetic look at Wallace is Stephen Lesher, *George Wallace: American Populist* (Boston: Addison-Wesley, 1993). See also, *Earl Black, Southern Governors and*

Civil Rights: Racial Segregation as a Campaign Issue in the Second Reconstruction (Boston: Harvard University, 1976). This is a look at the impact of the civil rights movement on southern politics. Another look is Michael R. Belknap, *Federal Law and Southern Order: Racial Violence and Constitutional Conflict in the Post-Brown South* (Athens: University of Georgia, 1987).

INDEX